1968

Rick Griffin *Joint show* 1967 lithograph

Cover: **Martin Sharp** *Jimi Hendrix* 1968 enamel on synthetic polymer film

1968

Michael Desmond and Christine Dixon

National Gallery of Australia
Distributed by Thames and Hudson

Edited, designed, typeset and produced by the Publications
Department, National Gallery of Australia, Canberra
Colour Separations by Prepress Services (WA) Pty Ltd, Perth
Printed in Australia by Lamb Printers Pty Ltd, Perth

National Library of Australia
Cataloguing-in-Publication data

Desmond, Michael, 1950–
1968
Includes index
ISBN 0 642 13037 X
1. Art — Political aspects — Exhibitions. 2. Art — Social
aspects — Exhibitions. 3. Art, Modern — 20th century —
Exhibitions. I. Dixon, Christine, II. National Gallery of
Australia. III. Title.

709.046074947

This catalogue is published on the occasion of an
exhibition held at the National Gallery of Australia,
29 July – 29 October 1995

Distributed by:
Thames and Hudson (Australia) Pty Ltd
11 Central Boulevard, Portside Business Park,
Port Melbourne, Victoria 3207, Australia

Thames and Hudson Ltd
30-34 Bloomsbury Street, London WC1B 3QP, UK

Thames and Hudson Inc
500 Fifth Avenue, New York, NY 10110, USA

ISBN in USA 0 500 97433 0
Library of Congress 95-61180

Acknowledgments

The authors wish to thank all their colleagues at the
National Gallery of Australia, particularly Kate Davidson,
Mary Eagle and fellow curators of the Departments of
Aboriginal Art, Australian Art and International Art; the
Photographic Services Department and Richard Pedvin;
Public Access and Peter Naumann; Publications and
Marketing, Suzanna Campbell, Kirsty Morrison,
Shirley Purchase and Theresa Willsteed; and the staff of the
National Gallery Research Library. Gratitude for their support
is extended to Anthony Ashbolt, to Peter Dixon, and to
Peta Jones.

Apologia

It may seem perverse, in an exhibition entitled *1968*, to
include artworks from 1967 and 1969 as well as the named
year. It appeared to us, however, that the meaning of 1968
extended to works produced in the two years which preceded
and succeeded it. We thought, in the spirit of the times, that a
show drawn from any single source such as the collection of
the National Gallery of Australia, Canberra, could afford to
stretch the boundaries of a mere calendar year.

MD/CD

Published with the assistance of *The Canberra Times*

Contents

1967

Carl Burton Stokes becomes Mayor of Cleveland, first black to be elected mayor of major US city / India and China border clashes / DNA synthesised / *Protest and Hope*, anti-Vietnam and civil rights works, on show at New School Art Center/ *L'art pour la paix au Vietnam* at Galerie Creuze, Paris / Charlotte Moorman arrested for indecent exposure while performing Nam June Paik's *Opera sextronique* / Pantyhose, paper dresses, the frug become fashionable / **JANUARY** 'Gathering of the tribes for a human be-in' led by Allen Ginsberg; 20,000 gather in Golden Gate Park, Haight-Ashbury, San Francisco / Apollo 1 catches fire, three astronauts killed / Students and workers demonstrate against Franco's regime in Madrid / **FEBRUARY** University unrest in Italy / Ronald Ryan hanged in Pentridge Prison, last execution in Australia / Bushfires in Tasmania, 21 dead / **MARCH** President Sukarno of Indonesia toppled / Tanker *Torrey Canyon* spills 100,000 tons of oil / **APRIL** 500,000 demonstrate in Spring mobilisation against Vietnam War / Military coup in Greece / **MAY** Biafra breaks away from Nigeria / Referendum on Australian Aboriginal rights gains 90% 'yes' vote / **JUNE** Six Day War; Israel defeats Egypt, Syria and Jordan / China explodes hydrogen bomb / Monterey Pop Festival / *Two Decades of American Painting* shown in Melbourne and Sydney / **JUNE–JULY** Race riots in Newark, Chicago, Nashville, Boston, Cincinnati, Detroit, Atlanta and elsewhere; 26 dead, 1500 injured, 1000 arrested / **JULY** John Newcombe wins Men's Singles at Wimbledon, Billie Jean King wins Women's Singles/ **AUGUST** Abbie Hoffman and others throw dollar bills onto floor of New York Stock Exchange/ **SEPTEMBER** First exhibition of *Arte povera* organised by Germano Celant in Genoa / **OCTOBER** Che Guevara killed by Bolivian army / 250,000 demonstrate outside Pentagon/ 'Death of Hippy' parade in Haight-Ashbury / Feminist group 'Radical Women' formed in New York / **DECEMBER** Successful first flight of British–French supersonic Concorde / Heart transplant operation in Cape Town, South Africa, performed by Dr Christiaan Barnard/ Youth International Party (Yippies) formed / Australian Prime Minister Harold Holt disappears, feared drowned

1968

US Presidential election campaign / Kassel: 4th Documenta includes Minimal artists / The Hague: First *Minimal art* exhibition in Europe, travels to Düsseldorf and Berlin / Riots at 34th Venice Biennale / Waterbed invented / Arthur Ashe wins US Open tennis championship/ Civil unrest increases in Northern Ireland / **JANUARY** John Gorton becomes Prime Minister of Australia / US spy ship *Pueblo* seized by North Korea, crew interned / Vietcong and North Vietnamese army launch Tet offensive in Saigon and 30 other South Vietnamese cities; US Embassy occupied; Hue besieged / **FEBRUARY** The Beatles retreat to ashram in India to study transcendental meditation with the Maharishi Mahesh Yogi / Hue recaptured/ Lionel Rose wins World Bantamweight boxing title / **MARCH** My Lai massacre of Vietnamese civilians by US soldiers (suppressed) / President Lyndon B. Johnson announces he will not run for re-election / Student unrest in Warsaw / **APRIL** Martin Luther King assassinated in Memphis; race riots spread to 125 cities / Student leader Rudi Dutschke shot and wounded in Munich; riots follow / *Hair* and *Boys in the Band* open on Broadway / **MAY** 30,000 students clash with police in Paris / Famine in Biafra /

Vietnam peace talks begin in Paris / Art critic Harold Greenberg visits Australia / **MAY–JUNE** Student uprising in Paris and across France; general strike / **JUNE** Robert Kennedy assassinated in Los Angeles / Andy Warhol shot and wounded by Valerie Solanas of SCUM (Society for Cutting Up Men) / Student riots in Yugoslavia, Japan and elsewhere/ De Gaulle government re-elected in landslide / Pierre Trudeau becomes Prime Minister of Canada / **JULY** Police attack student anti-war demonstrators in Sydney and Melbourne / Pope Paul VI rejects artificial birth control for Catholics / **AUGUST** Invasion of Czechoslovakia by Warsaw Pact countries / Democratic Party Convention in Chicago disrupted by peace protestors; police riot ensues / Joh Bjelke-Petersen becomes Premier of Queensland / National Gallery of Victoria, Melbourne re-opens in new building with *The Field* exhibition of contemporary Australian art / **SEPTEMBER** Walter De Maria exhibits dirt at Munich gallery / *Prospekt '68* shown at the Kunsthalle, Düsseldorf, one of the earliest exhibitions of Conceptual art / Feminists protest against Miss America pageant in Atlantic City / **OCTOBER** Mexico City Olympic Games; Black Power salute by US athletes Tommie Smith and John Carlos / Mass anti-war demonstrations in Washington / Marcel Duchamp dies / **NOVEMBER** Richard Nixon elected US President / Rain Lover wins the Melbourne Cup / **DECEMBER** General strike in Italy

1969

Golda Meir elected Prime Minister of Israel / Yasser Arafat elected Chairman of the Palestine Liberation Organisation / Mao Tse-Tung ends Chinese Cultural Revolution; Red Guards disbanded / Trial of Chicago Eight / Judy Chicago and Miriam Shapiro announce the *First Feminist Art Program* at the California Institute of Arts / *First National Conference on Women's Liberation* in Chicago / Human *in vitro* fertilisation / Concorde: Supersonic passenger flight / Microprocessor invented / Rod Laver wins Tennis Grand Slam — Australian, French, US Opens and Wimbledon / **JANUARY** Civil rights marches in Belfast/ **MARCH** John Lennon and Yoko Ono honeymoon at the Amsterdam Hilton with a 'bed-in for peace' / *When Attitudes Become Form*, seminal exhibition of Conceptual art, opens in Bern, later travels to Krefeld and London / **APRIL** Radical art group, the Art Workers Coalition, founded in New York / Charles de Gaulle resigns, succeeded as President of France by Georges Pompidou / **JUNE** Stonewall riot in New York marks birth of Gay Liberation / **JULY** Apollo II astronauts Neil Armstrong and Edwin 'Buzz' Aldrin land on moon / First pull-out of US troops from Vietnam / **AUGUST** Woodstock festival in Bethel, NY; approximately 400,000 people attend / US terrorist group 'Weathermen' begins bombing campaign with the slogan 'Bring the war home' / British troops sent to Northern Ireland / the Charles Manson murders / **SEPTEMBER** Ho Chi Minh dies / Willy Brandt forms Social Democratic government in Germany / **OCTOBER** Vietnam Moratorium demonstrations / **NOVEMBER** My Lai massacre revealed / In USA 250,000 demonstrate against Vietnam War, *Parade of the dead* stretches for 8km / Native Americans occupy Alcatraz Island / **DECEMBER** First passenger flight of Jumbo jet (Seattle–New York City) / Violence at Altamont Rock Festival in California; Hell's Angels employed as security guards kill one fan, two others die, 700 injured

WOODSTOCK
MUSIC & ART FAIR

presents

AN
AQUARIAN
EXPOSITION

in

WHITE LAKE, N.Y.*

3 DAYS of PEACE & MUSIC

AUGUST 15, 16, 17.

WITH

FRI., AUG. 15
Joan Baez
Arlo Guthrie
Tim Hardin
Richie Havens
Incredible String Band
Ravi Shankar
Sly And The Family Stone
Bert Sommer
Sweetwater

SAT., AUG. 16
Canned Heat
Creedence Clearwater
Grateful Dead
Keef Hartley
Janis Joplin
Jefferson Airplane
Mountain
Quill
Santana
The Who

SUN., AUG. 17
The Band
Jeff Beck Group
Blood, Sweat and Tears
Joe Cocker
Crosby, Stills and Nash
Jimi Hendrix
Iron Butterfly
Ten Years After
Johnny Winter

ART SHOW

CRAFTS BAZAAR

FOOD

HUNDREDS OF ACRES
TO ROAM ON

MUSIC STARTS AT 4:00 P.M. ON
FRIDAY, AND AT 1:00 P.M. ON
SATURDAY AND SUNDAY

*White Lake, Town of Bethel, Sullivan County, N.Y.

The sacred,
that is the enemy

graffiti, Paris, May '68

1968

The year 1968 signals many changes in culture, society and politics. Rebellion erupted around the world. In Paris, Prague, Chicago, Mexico City, in China, Australia and in Latin America, many people believed that a new day was dawning. Not the old days, not the tired politics of the Cold War, but an altered consciousness would prevail.

The arts were one battleground of this new struggle. Idealism came to the forefront for the first time for many decades. Instead of the old bastions of capitalism and communism, there was a new feeling of experiment, of trying out extremes — in art, music, theatre, in everyday life and personal relations, as in politics.

1968 marked the replacement of painting as the most important carrier of visual meaning. A clenched fist, the peace sign, the symbol of the Vietnam Moratorium campaign, all seemed to challenge the social and political torpor of high art with its quiescent museums. Instead of concurring with accepted cultural standards, artists could see a new arena of endeavour, implying constant experiments and an obsession with originality.

The avant-garde tradition of high art continued however, seemingly undisturbed by the social and cultural changes of the sixties. New movements succeeded each other like product brand names — Op, Pop, Minimal, Conceptual, Earth art — while artists of older styles, like Post-painterly Abstraction or Hard-edge, sailed on regardless. But there was an undercurrent of discontent.

The flickerings of experimental film and video pointed one way to the future. Such phenomena as environments, happenings, conceptualism, the use of photographic imagery,

the triumph of text, and above all of sculpture as a real, material event or process, seemed to show that static painting was dead.

In the twentieth century, for the first time, visual artists were no longer bearers of moral and ethical meaning for the community. In the West (North America, Europe and Australia) the old guard protected an academy of 'pure values' which no longer meant anything to most people in terms of aesthetics. Almost everybody under thirty — a majority of the population — reacted to popular music as the heartbeat of the times. Instead of paintings, popular posters and record covers were the vernacular.

Sentimental appeals to the unifying values of nation or class no longer sufficed. Images of some individuals appealed to millions: Che Guevara, Ho Chi Minh, Martin Luther King, Janis Joplin and Malcolm X spoke to many who felt their vague aspirations to liberty had never been voiced in parliament, and never would be. Previously hidden elements, minorities in a conformist society, surfaced. The once covert 'sex and drugs' lifestyle of rock musicians became public, and was coupled to the appeal of their music, a thing to envy rather than censure. Martin Sharp portrayed *Jimi Hendrix* 1968 as an explosion of light and colour, the personification of rock's energy.

Students took over the universities to teach their professors how things should be done. 'Law and order' began to mean repression to a proportionately greater part of the population. Previously silent voices called out for equality before the law: black power and women's liberation renewed themselves in the sixties, while the green movement, access for the disabled, and campaigns for indigenous people's rights were born, and gay liberation emerged to challenge the status quo.

Visual artists, like the politicians, were left groping in the dark. Painting on canvas or sculpting in bronze were no longer

Arnold Skolnick *3 days of peace & music* 1969 screenprint

Mexico City, October 1968: Tommie Smith and John Carlos give the Black Power salute at the Olympic Games (Popperfoto)

Wesley Stacey *No title (Anti-Vietnam War march)* 1967
gelatin silver photograph

adequate in this world of fast-moving television imagery, advertising, movies, drive-ins, demonstrations, and all the other triumphs of instant imagery. The concerns of 1968 — social justice, political equality, feminism, ecology, the fight against racism, the struggle for cultural specificity — can be seen echoing into the 1990s.

It seems obvious now, even to the point of not stating it, that culture and society are intertwined in a continuing process of transformation. But politicians in conservative societies resisted any call for change. The world was still divided into peculiar spheres of influence, frozen into Cold War alliances of fear and hatred. The Soviet Union dominated the nations of Eastern Europe while the United States yet believed in the Monroe Doctrine, which gave North Americans economic and political control of Central and South America. The atom bomb ruled as the ultimate tool to manipulate the fate of the world.

The ruling oligarchies of Europe which had survived the cataclysmic battles of the Second World War still ruled over their colonies in Africa and Asia. Britain, Belgium and the Netherlands began to grant independence to some of 'their' territories (Singapore, Kenya, Uganda, Zambia, Zaire, Rwanda, Indonesia) in the fifties and sixties, while France and

Yousuf Karsh *The Apollo 11 crew: Astronauts Neil Armstrong, Edwin Aldrin, Michael Collins* 1969 gelatin silver photograph

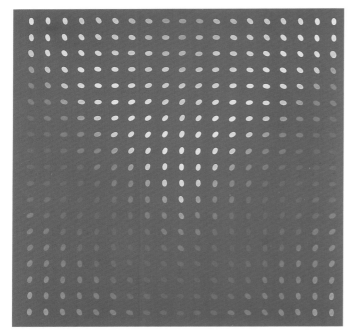

Bridget Riley *D* from *Nineteen greys* 1968 screenprint

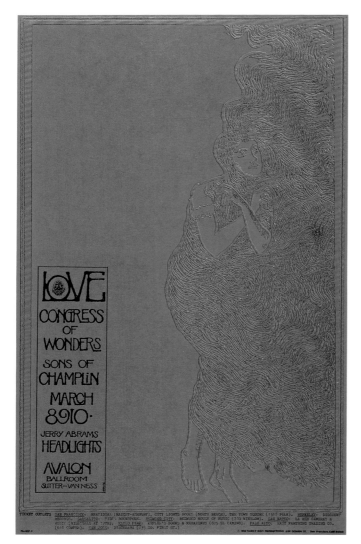

Stanley Mouse *Love/Congress of Wonders/Sons of Champlin* 1968
lithograph

Portugal refused (Algeria, Vietnam, Tahiti, Martinique, Angola, Mozambique, East Timor).

The 'Third World' became a political reality in the sixties, aligned to neither the capitalist nor the communist bloc. The resistance of the colonised extended to dispossessed minority peoples: in Northern Ireland, in the Palestinian resistance, in Iron Curtain countries such as Czechoslovakia, in the unrest of native Americans and Aboriginal Australians. The centre and the periphery were beginning to realign. Those who did not protest were rapidly becoming 'the silent majority' and the rest went 'underground', were seen as dissenters, or belonged to the counter culture.

In the past, uprisings against the ruling social and political order occurred when times were hard. Hunger, poverty and oppression were the sparks that lit the flames of revolt. But 1968 was different. The students who rose up against their governments were richer and more privileged than any rebels of the past. In France, in May '68, the children of the bourgeoisie were joined by industrial workers in an alliance unknown since the French Revolution of 1789. Dissatisfied intellectuals again joined with the masses in confronting the established order.

When students revolted in France, Italy, Mexico City and the United States in the summer of 1968, the authorities were petrified. What was happening here? Could ordinary people object to the rulers, as had the 'colonies'? Would they rebel? 'There's something happening here, what it is ain't exactly clear', Buffalo Springfield sang in 1967.[1]

Artists, too, were perplexed. The values that came to the forefront of visual art embraced new ideas — the technology of mass photography, television, photocopying, film, and intervention with the earth itself — which were prized above traditional, individualist artistic values for the first time. Painting became three-dimensional, sculpture retreated onto the page, and popular imagery triumphed.

It is now that artists consciously tried to enter the community, to appeal to the mass audiences of rock concerts and political demonstrations. In the 1960s British and American Pop artists thought that they had embraced the meaning of their age by incorporating the techniques of mass advertising into their art. Brashness, repetition and photography allowed Andy Warhol, Roy Lichtenstein, Robert Rauschenberg, Joe Tilson, Richard Hamilton and R. B. Kitaj, among others, a foothold into popular culture.

But the social and political upheavals of the late 1960s showed that Pop artists, especially in the United States and in Great Britain, were settled securely in the academy of high art. So how were the new circumstances of permanent revolution to be incorporated?

Michael Johnson *Frontal red* 1969 synthetic polymer paint on shaped canvas

Unknown artist *Easy rider* 1969 photolithograph

FILMS AND TELEVISION

1967
In the Heat of the Night / Bonnie and Clyde / The Graduate / Up the Down Staircase / Valley of the Dolls / Elvira Madigan / Thoroughly Modern Millie / To Sir With Love / The Dirty Dozen / You Only Live Twice / Guess Who's Coming to Dinner? / Cool Hand Luke / Belle de Jour / La Chinoise / Accident / Far From Vietnam

1968
2001: A Space Odyssey / Bullitt / Planet of the Apes / The Producers / Rosemary's Baby / The Thomas Crown Affair / I Love You, Alice B. Toklas / Yellow Submarine/ If / Lonesome Cowboys / The Green Berets / Romeo and Juliet / Petulia / Faces / Wild in the Streets

1969
Midnight Cowboy / Alice's Restaurant / Easy Rider / Medium Cool / The Wild Bunch / Bob & Carol & Ted & Alice / Butch Cassidy and the Sundance Kid / Love Story / Z / Satyricon / One plus One – Sympathy for the Devil / The Damned / You Can't See Round Corners / Two Thousand Weeks / Don't Look Back / O What a Lovely War

TOP-RATING TV PROGRAMS
1968

Sydney
(1) The Fugitive
(2) The Champions
(3) Bandstand
(4) The Flying Nun
(5) News and Weather

Melbourne
(1) Homicide
(2) Till Death Us Do Part
(3) Channel 9 Theatre
(4) Daktari
(5) Showcase '68

TUESDAY
MAY 21, 1968—EVENING VIEWING, 7 PM TO CLOSE

WIN4 — WOLLONGONG
Relaying to WIN11 Moruya

7.00 I DREAM OF JEANNIE
Fastest Gun In The West. While Tony watches a TV Western, he longs for the days when a man had to be strong to survive Jeannie blinks and Tony finds he is a U.S. Marshal in a frontier town. Stars **Barbara Eden** and **Larry Hagman.**

7.30 FRED ASTAIRE SPECIAL
Fred Astaire dances his way from yesterday's nostalgia to today's scene with guests **Barrie Chase, Simon and Garfunkel, Sergio Mendes and Brazil 66, Gordian Knot, the Young Holt Trio, and Neal Hefti's Orchestra.**

8.25 ROVING EYE

8.30 THE FUGITIVE
Ten Thousand Pieces Of Silver. An Indiana newspaper publisher offers $10,000 for the capture of Richard Kimble and he is spotted by a store keeper after the reward. Stars **David Janssen** as Dr. Richard Kimble. **A.**

9.30 TONIGHT SHOW
Variety program hosted by John Laws and featuring guest stars.

11.00 LATE NEWS

11.15 EPILOGUE

11.20 CLOSE

Page 48—TV WEEK

NBN3 — NEWCASTLE

7.00 BEWITCHED
Toys In Babeland. Urgently summoned to the Taj Mahal, Endora leaves little Tabatha in the care of a baby-sitter, hastily created from the ranks of her toys. and the youngster seizes the chance to demonstrate her growing command of the occult arts. Stars **Dick York, Elizabeth Montgomery** and **Agnes Moorehead.**

7.30 FRED ASTAIRE SPECIAL
Fred Astaire dances his way from yesterday's nostalgia to today's scene with guests **Barrie Chase, Simon and Garfunkel, Sergio Mendes and Brazil 66, the Young Holt Trio, Gordian Knot and Neal Hefti's Orchestra.**

8.30 ROVING EYE

8.35 MOTHERS-IN-LAW
[DEBUT] Comedy series starring **Eve Arden** and **Kaye Ballard.**

9.05 MY NAME'S McGOOLEY — WHAT'S YOURS?
Would You Believe A Gipsy, Well Would You? Rita invites a teacup reader around to the house to predict the future of the family. Stars **Gordon Chater, Judi Farr** and **John Meillon.**

9.35 TWELVE O'CLOCK HIGH
The Hunters And The Killers. Stars **Paul Burke. A.**

10.35 ARMCHAIR THEATRE
A.

11.30 MEDITATION

11.35 CLOSE

ABC-TV
RELAYING TO ALL NSW COUNTRY ABC STATIONS

7.00 NEWS, NEWSREEL AND WEATHER

7.30 THIS DAY TONIGHT
Daily public affairs program linking Sydney, Melbourne, Canberra and regionals concerned with the news and events of the day.

8.00 BAT OUT OF HELL
It seems to Mark Paxton and Diana Stuart that their plot to murder the latter's wealthy husband is foolproof. Starring **Dudley Foster, Sylvia Sims** and **John Thaw. A.**

8.27 NEWS

8.30 TILL DEATH US DO PART
Claustrophobia. Going on holiday, the Garnetts drive down to the west of England, with Alf displaying an independent approach to road rules. They take over a lonely cottage and the countryside will never be quite the same again. Stars **Warren Mitchell, Una Stubbs, Anthony Booth** and **Dandy Nichols. A.**

9.00 IMPACT
The Edge Of The Outback. Portrait of life in a typical town and surrounding area. Filmed in Queensland.

9.50 NEWS AND WEATHER

10.00 RUGBY

11.00 CLOSE

ATN7

7.00 THE FLYING NUN
Cyrano De Bertrille. Pedro a San Juan shopkeeper, asks Sister Bertrille to write love letters for him but she declares his plan to be dishonest and insists that he learn to read and write so that he may carry on the correspondence himself. Thirty-minute comedy series starring **Sally Field** as Sister Bertrille, a young novice who not only puts her foot in her mouth every time she opens it but finds she cannot keep either foot on the ground when a strong gust of wind blows and catches the brim of her cornette. Co-stars **Alejandro Rey** and **Marge Redmond.**

7.30 FRED ASTAIRE SPECTACULAR
Fred Astaire stars in this special nominated for an Emmy award. Spectacular production numbers include the classic "Top Hat" sequence. Guest stars include **Barrie Chase, Gordian Knot, Simon and Garfunkle, the Young Holt Trio, Sergio Mendez and Brazil 66** and the **Neal Hefti Orchestra.**

8.30 MOVIE
The Beat Generation (1959). A detective is assigned to track down a crazed rapist whose pattern of crime has included several attacks on the wives of policemen. He becomes so obsessed with his investigation that he soon believes his own wife, expecting a baby, has also been a victim of assault and that the child will not be his. Stars **Steve Cochran, Mamie Van Doren, Ray Anthony, Louis Armstrong** and **Maggie Hayes. AO.**

10.20 SUNBALL COMPETITION
With Rex Mossop.

10.25 RUGBY LEAGUE
Replay.

11.45 CLOSE

TCN9

7.00 DICK VAN DYKE
Washington Versus The Bunny. Rob is tortured by a dream that he's a puppet for Laura whom he wakes, determined to put his foot down. Stars **Dick Van Dyke, Mary Tyler Moore, Rose Marie** and **Morey Amsterdam.**

7.30 STAR TREK
The Deadly Years. A weird disease attacks Kirk, Scott and McCoy when they visit the strange planet called Gamma Hydra Four. The disease increases their bodily ageing processes to an incredible rate. Starring **William Shatner, Leonard Nimoy, James Doohan, DeForest Kelley, Charles Drake** and **Sarah Marshall. A.**

8.27 NEWS HEADLINES

8.30 THE FUGITIVE
The End Is But The Beginning. Kimble picks up a hitch-hiker while working as a truck driver and soon afterwards is involved in an accident. The hitch-hiker is killed and Kimble decides to try to convince Lt. Gerard that he was killed so that Gerard will finally give up the chase. Starring **David Janssen** and **Barry Morse. A.**

9.27 NEWS HEADLINES

9.30 THE TONIGHT SHOW
Variety show with John Laws.

11.00 LATE NEWS

11.15 IT IS WRITTEN
Religious program.

11.45 PETER GUNN
Short Motive. Stars **Craig Stevens. A.**

12.10 VIEWPOINT

12.15 CLOSE

TEN10

7.00 THE MARRIAGE GAME
Compered by Malcolm Searle.

7.30 GARRISON'S GORILLAS
Breakout. Garrison is set the task of rescuing a Resistance leader from a German prison, and when the first attempt fails, he plays a dangerous hand in which the governor's son is the trump card. Stars **Ron Harper, Cesare Danova, Brendon Boone, Rudy Salari** and **Chris Carey.**

8.30 CANDID CAMERA

9.00 PERSONALITY SQUARES
Compered by Joe Martin.

9.30 TELESCOPE
John Bailey and Norm Benneli and the team look at current affairs.

10.00 HERE'S HARRY
The Daily Help. Harry's housekeeper, Mrs. Williams, goes to live in Bournemouth and his efforts to find a suitable replacement throw Woodbridge Domestic Agency into confusion.

10.30 GUNSMOKE
Moonstone. A reformed outlaw lives quietly near Dodge City with his feeblemindled brother, but shadows from the past fall across both their lives. Stars **James Arness**, with guests **Michael Kellin** and **Tom Skerritt. AO.**

11.00 STARS IN ACTION
Well Of Anger. With marriage in mind, young farmer, Ed Sawyer, builds a homestead on his drought stricken land, but his bride-to-be cannot understand his reluctance to fight for his water rights and the wedding bells ring fainter as the days go by. Starring **Nancy Gates** and **Bill Williams. A.**

12.00 CLOSE

TV WEEK—Page 49

Pages 48–49 from *TV WEEK* 21 May 1968 (Pacific Publications Pty Ltd)

Don't free me,
I'll do it myself

graffiti, Paris, May '68

Public and private

Art was no longer a private act — it was public. For some artists, especially Eva Hesse and Robert Morris, the work of art was dependent on the changing experience of the viewer. The making of art was on show as much as any completed object. Art was not only concerned with ends; it was primarily a matter of process, to do with transformation, and thus the concept of transcendence arose.

Morris's felt seems to breathe, Hesse's latex and fabric structures dematerialise before our eyes, relying on capricious breezes that move their component parts on suspension lines in each installation. Hesse's *Contingent* 1969, suspended by all but invisible cords from above, literally depends on its resistance against the earth. Sculptors in the late 1960s often used non-industrial substances to make their artworks, like the German guru Joseph Beuys's reliance on natural materials such as wool (felt), wood, fat and rubber.

An opposite, mainly geometrical tendency appears in the work of the purist, abstract artists of Op, Minimal, Hard-edge and Colour-field movements such as Bridget Riley, Sol LeWitt and Nigel Lendon. Here is an attempt to reach for ultimate abstract intellectual values: pure colour, pure mathematics and pure proportion. The metaphor is architecture, as the spatial relationships of modernist buildings and public places are reiterated. Within the intimacy of a gallery space, the large scale and repetition often disconcert the viewer.

By going to such extremes in an effort to attain the ultimate goal of visual perfection, artists risked alienating any appeal to popular audiences. New technologies were tried — plastic-coated metal, steel mesh, or layers of laminex. Hostility has always been an important value for modernist art: the viewer's comfort is not desired.

In other spheres, it was new social verities that mattered. Simple recording was not enough, as private and public worlds collided. Diane Arbus uses her freshness of eye to look at contemporary America anew. She captures the small-town values of the 4th of July parade, the perversion of the star-spangled banner manacled to the military adventure in Vietnam, while at the same time observing the desperation and courage of everyday black American experience. As a high art, or fine art photographer, however, she presented it to mostly white viewers.

For the first time in history perhaps, it is urban life which is normal experience for most people. Joyce Allen shows high-rise flats — a suburban norm for Australia. These had hardly been represented in the past. In *Up and down* 1968, lack of privacy allows quirks and oddities to appear from under the mundane surface of any city.

For Kevin Gilbert, this is the time to represent the Aboriginal experience. What is *Christmas Eve in the land of the dispossessed* 1969 but another opportunity for justice let slip? In 1967, in a historic referendum of the white electorate, an overwhelming majority of non-Aboriginal Australian voters recognised that it was manifestly unfair not to allow indigenous Australians to vote, nor to be citizens of their own country.

Linocut, the simple graphic means which these artists used to communicate their ideas, highlights the visual schizophrenia of simplicity and complexity which has come to characterise our times. The ideas of 1968 divide the contemporary era from the postwar age. The world wars which had arisen from ancient European hatreds were now fading from view, known to rising generations only from old newsreels.

Diane Arbus *Boy with a straw hat waiting to march in a pro-war parade, N.Y.C., 1967* 1967 gelatin silver photograph

Kevin Gilbert *Christmas Eve in the land of the dispossessed* 1969, printed 1990 linocut

Joyce Allen *Up and down* 1968 linocut

An individual's actions could speak to many not involved in the actual events that took place. *Hasta la victoria siempre* [*Until the final victory*] 1968 needs only a photographic silhouette to evoke Che Guevara, the Latin American revolutionary. Born in Argentina, part of the Cuban uprising, killed in Bolivia in 1967, he was more than a continental or Third World figure — he was admired by youth around the world. Che's head, outlined in purple, reverberates against the clear yellow background of Alfredo Rostgaard's film poster.

Radical ideas appealed across national boundaries. Rebellion against the established order means different things in different societies. The complacency of Anglo-European polities was challenged by the very concept of youthful change. So for Che, the Cuban Revolution could be exported to Bolivia, adopting the Maoist idea of permanent revolution. While his venture was unsuccessful in military and political terms, it came to stand for a global transformation of values.

Joe Tilson repeats a disturbing image of the dead revolutionary, the photograph of Che's body released by the Bolivian military to prove to the world that he was dead at last. The artist casually superimposes a crumpled snapshot found on his body. It shows Tania, his lover and revolutionary partner, in a rare moment of leisure. Personal mementoes become public property in our mass media age. Marshall

Alfredo Rostgaard *Hasta la victoria siempre* (*Until the final victory*) 1968 screenprint

Joe Tilson *T — Tania la guerillera* from *A–Z box ... fragments of an oneiric alphabet ...* 1969–70 photo-screenprint, collage

McLuhan invented the concept of the 'global village' just in time to explain the phenomenon.

The very language of visual images changed. For speculative young people, psychedelic drugs meant new perceptions of colour and pattern. In San Francisco, poster artists publicising rock music concerts created a new, vibrant language, echoed in the lightshows and visual effects used at the shows. Wes Wilson and Victor Moscoso, among others, used the dissonances of purple and acid orange, blue and lime green, red and lemon yellow, in their rainbow printings of drawn and photographic images. These were combined with all-but-illegible lettering to produce brilliant announcements for the renaissance of live concerts in the television era.

Posters and record covers were the visual idiom for an entire generation. For high art, the challenge was unique, especially for the Pop artists of the early sixties who prided themselves on their radical capture of the images of mass culture and advertising. At the end of the decade, Jasper Johns revives a myth of his American youth in *High school days* 1969 — a shoe with mirrored toe, cast in lead relief. Hidden sexuality is revealed, with polished shoes used for looking up girls' skirts.

In Britain in 1968, Patrick Caulfield purifies and glorifies the banal rectangles of the café sign, a loudspeaker, and bathroom mirrors. Allen Jones presents simple-minded views of sexual relations in *Life class* 1968, with 'woman' as the receiver of male desire. Robert Rauschenberg tries to engage the difficulties of modern life in complex, layered views of political assassination and the space race.

New areas of representation were being claimed by artists who felt themselves to be part of the political and social struggles of the day. The fight against racism spread from the fringes of black and left-wing communities at the beginning of the decade to a central place in society's consciousness. In the late 1960s there arose new waves of feminism and environmental activism, and the gay liberation movement was born. Some artists identified the new issues: Vivienne Binns confronted a complacent Australia with the vibrant sexual politics of *Vag dens* 1967. There were novel threats to the status quo here.

19

Patrick Caulfield *Café sign* 1968 screenprint

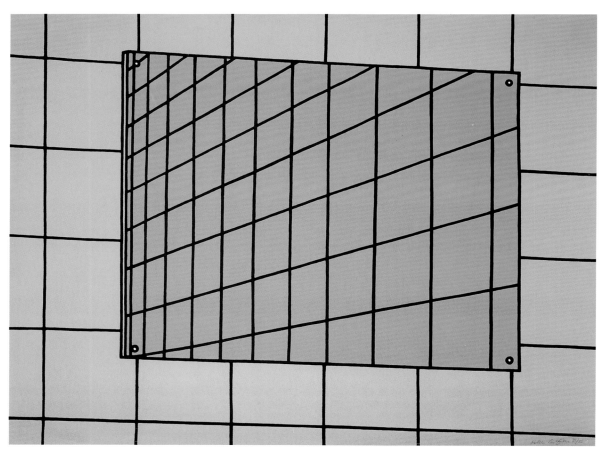

Patrick Caulfield *Bathroom mirror* 1968 screenprint

Lee Conklin (Herb Greene, photographer) Poster for *Grateful Dead/Pentangle/Sir Douglas Quintet* 1969 lithograph

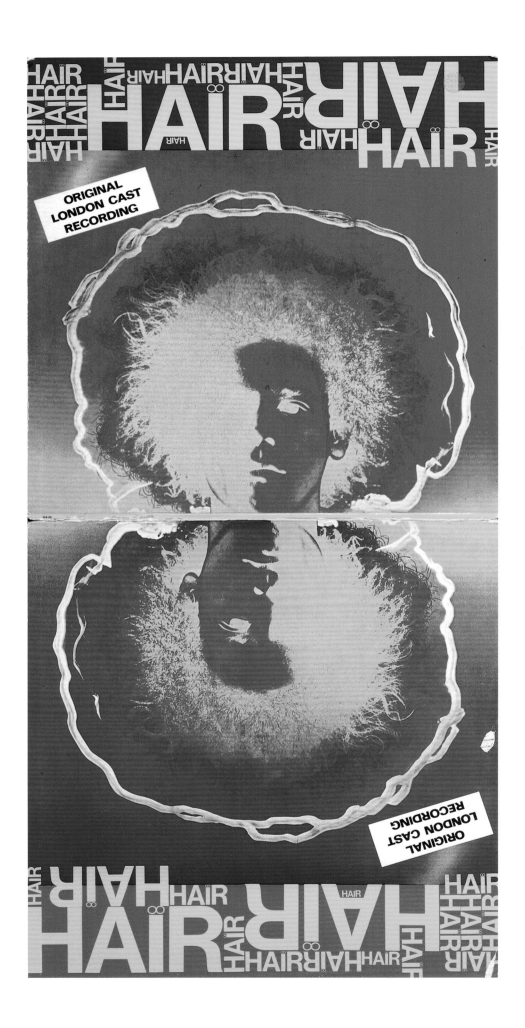

Poetry is in
the streets

graffiti, Paris, May '68

Art on the streets

A new theatre emerged in the 1960s: the theatre of the streets, of demonstrations and happenings. Drama combined with visual art in political and cultural events that blurred the boundaries of genre. Art came out of the galleries onto the streets, where the action was. Public spaces became important venues for art.

Performance art was an attempt to find new cultural experiences. From the 1950s artists such as John Cage, Allan Kaprow and the Gutai group staged mixed-media 'happenings' which could involve the audience. Art was no longer a separate domain inhabited only by its practitioners; it was an arena for all those who were engaged in the transformation of contemporary society.

Politics and culture were inseparable, as Abbie Hoffman and his followers showed in Wall Street in April 1967. They disrupted the New York Stock Exchange by scattering dollar bills from the balcony onto the trading floor. The Exchange had to close. This symbolic performance revealed the essence of capitalist activity — a mad scramble for money.

By 1968 it seemed essential that the group be recognised as more significant than its component parts. The rock musical *Hair* is remembered for ensemble effects, such as the whole cast naked on stage, rather than for star performers. *Hair* encompassed not only mystic references to the zodiac, but also the values of pacifism and the birth of a new optimism:

> When the moon is in the Seventh House
> And Jupiter aligns with Mars,
> Then peace will rule the planets
> And love will rule the stars.
> It is the dawning of the age of Aquarius ...[2]

Paris, May '68: an uprising of students and workers made the French government tremble. Art students joined their colleagues in protests against their authoritarian, outdated educational institutions. Leaning towards the Maoist example in China, European student leaders saw an immediate need to involve the workers in their struggle.

In their co-operative workshops, art students produced hundreds of copies of simple screenprinted posters. They thought of this work as combining art and politics in a new, vital way. In the spirit of collaboration and egalitarianism which prevailed at this time, no one claimed individual credit for the posters that were produced. They were pasted up everywhere, on the streets and in the metros, in the factories and the universities. The posters were technically crude, usually printed in one colour onto cheap butcher's paper. Some very powerful images resulted from these limited means of expression.

The police and other armed forces were obvious symbols of repression. A gendarme's hat is outlined in black, with *No!* being authority's reaction to any request for freedom or for change. *No!* is also the automatic response of the rebels to the armed power of the state. Photographs were used in combination with drawings and lettering, as in the surrealist rendering of the policeman with a tear-gas canister for a head. It was printed, not in strident red or strong black, but in pink.

These simple representations are more successful in aesthetic terms than the slickest, most sophisticated advertising billboards. They are memorable. President Charles de Gaulle, revered as the leader of the French government-in-exile in the Second World War, stands as a caricature with outstretched arms and military hat. *Le chienlit c'est lui!* [*He's the freak!*] echoes the arrogant pronouncement of another French dictator, Louis XIV: 'L'état c'est moi' [I am the state]. The irreverence with which symbols of authority such as de Gaulle and the police are treated has a long history in France, from Daumier onwards. It always leaves the bourgeoisie discomfited. The art of May '68 was public, unauthorised and anonymous, a libertarian tradition revived.

Hair Original London cast recording 1968, Polydor

Unknown artists *No!, No!, He's the freak!,The situation is easing, People's power YES* screenprints 1968

Paris, May 1968: Student demonstration (J P Rey/Gamma/Picture media)

The most important concept in the French uprising of 1968 was inclusion: there are images of people demonstrating together in *People's power YES*, and in the childlike silhouette of a factory captioned *Support the occupation of the factories*. Strikes at the state-owned Renault plants and elsewhere threatened the nation's economy, while running battles in the streets challenged the sacred cow of 'law and order'. Anarchy, disorder and the breakdown of social order were ends for which the revolutionaries strived.

If, as Daniel Cohn-Bendit (Danny the Red) argued, the current regime were morally bankrupt, then an egalitarian reorganisation of society was both desirable and urgently necessary. The gradualism of social democrats in capitalist parliamentary democracies was compromised by continued right-wing rule and by fascist elements in the police and the army. These became a prime target for dissenters.

The artworkers of the *Atelier Populaire* [People's or Popular Studio] saw the ORTF, the French state monopoly of radio and television, as the enemy. It was the apparatus of electronic state control of the masses. Connections with the spies of the French security forces were revealed in *The police speak to you every evening at 8 p.m.* A helmeted figure lurks behind every ORTF microphone. In some ways May '68 was the first TV revolution, as the Vietnam War was the first TV war.

Political action on the streets could also be a subject for art. Wesley Stacey photographed an anti-Vietnam War demonstration in Australia in 1967. He used the technique of tone drop-out to remove most shades of grey from the image. This emphasises the strong lettering on banners and placards, to make images and ideas speak in black and white. The slightly staid appearance of the student protesters would be transformed in the next couple of years, as passions rose and lifestyles changed.

For the British artist Joe Tilson, it was appropriate to use mass media images of the tanks from the Soviet Union and other Warsaw Pact countries which invaded Czechoslovakia in August 1968. Jan Palach was a young Prague student who set himself on fire in Wenceslas Square. His spectacular individual protest came to symbolise the nation's, and the freedom-loving world's, protest against the invasion. It echoed the famous suicide by self-immolation of a Vietnamese Buddhist monk in 1963.

Tilson took a reproduction of Jan Palach's photograph in a newspaper (itself taken from a portrait made for his family or for his school yearbook), complete with caption 'Jan Palach, suicide by fire, January 1969'. He placed it on the symbolic field of a flag or the rays of a halo, and attached this with paperclips to a montage of repeated photographic images of specific European and African conflicts. Ordinary Czechoslovakians throw stones at Russian tanks in the streets of Prague, while young African men line up for military service, presumably as volunteers in the almost-forgotten Biafran war in Nigeria. Some young people in every generation never grow old, victims of the military machine of

Joe Tilson *Jan Palach: Suicide by fire, January 1969* 1969 photolithograph, collage

war, patriotism and sacrifice. The dead youth Jan Palach will always be twenty years old.

This kind of art is very specific to its time, place, and to contemporary events. Those people engaged in the events of 1968 will always remember. If an image enters into the public imagination by repeated viewing, like the explosion of the mushroom cloud at Hiroshima, it can be alluded to, quoted or transformed by artists to enlarge the frame of reference, the repertory of iconic signs. Otherwise, the meaning dies.

Russian tanks on the streets of Prague, the death of the Czechoslovakian Spring, the fiery suicide of Jan Palach, were unforgettable for the generation that witnessed them on television in 1968. In the same way the man with the shopping bags challenging a tank in Beijing's Tiananmen Square in June 1989 has come to represent Chinese rebellion. But as communal memory banks are bombarded by more and more information, old images are displaced or never seen by later generations. What remains of the revolt of 1968?

Czechoslovakia, August 1968: Russian tanks on the streets of Prague (Camera Press)

Saigon, February 1968: Chief of police executes Vietcong suspect (Eddie Adams, AAP)

Happiness is a
new idea

graffiti, Paris, May '68

Seeing music

In the 1960s it was thought that the altered perceptions resulting from drug experience might aid artistic exploration. There were precedents, such as the use of opium by the nineteenth-century poets Coleridge and Baudelaire. Now the drug experience was available to anyone who accepted its personal, cultural, social or political justifications. The renowned British novelist Aldous Huxley published his influential testament *The Doors of Perception* in 1954. He had moved from Europe to the United States and then Mexico, to a new hemisphere, when the Second World War erupted in Europe at the end of the 1930s.

Like D. H. Lawrence, Huxley saw the new world of the Americas as a source of hope, not infected by centuries-old conflicts of nation, class and race. In order to expand his perceptions, he experimented with *peyote*, a naturally-occurring substance used by the Nahuatl peoples. Dr Timothy Leary, later known as the drug guru, was expelled from Harvard University in 1963 for subjecting students to unauthorised experiments. He advocated widespread use of LSD and other psychotropic chemicals to change experience. Leary's slogan, 'Tune in, turn on, drop out', advocated a non-political message of personal liberation from bourgeois values. LSD was legal in California until January 1967.

The visual distortions and enhancement of colour which resulted from drug use, especially marijuana and LSD, were seminal for psychedelic art in the late sixties. Poster artists in particular attempted to reproduce the 'mind-bending' effects of drugs in their works. Huxley's and Leary's individual and psychological arguments, which advocated an altered reality, coincided with new cultural, social and political movements in the late 1960s.

The explosion of dissent at this time meant that normative social reality, especially the bourgeois and authoritarian values of 'white bread' Western culture, were rejected by

a new generation. Young people, usually from middle-class backgrounds, became rebels when what they saw as harmless pleasures were censured and punished by the authorities. The police and state institutions were seen first as killjoys, and then as the enemy of youth culture.

By 1967 the main centre for acid rock was San Francisco, simmering in the so-called 'summer of love'. Music entrepreneur Bill Graham staged hundreds of concerts, with posters to advertise each one. His main venue was the Fillmore West, while the Family Dog Company's rival concerts were put on at the Avalon Ballroom. Artists were commissioned to produce advertising posters for each concert.

A startling new element in these posters was their vibrant colour. Artists and printers experimented with Day-glo inks, almost fluorescent in their effect. Brilliant orange and yellow, acid pink, sharp lime green, bright blue, red and purple were combined in free forms, without intermediary black outlines. Some posters were printed on foil paper, usually silver or gold. Others used fluorescent inks which glowed under ultra-violet light. Another technique was the 'rainbow roll' or 'split-fountain' effect, where bands of different-coloured inks merged to produce new combinations of colour.

Psychedelic graphic style, especially lettering, was derived from the European artists of *Art Nouveau* and *Jugendstil* at the turn of the century. Alphonse Mucha and Aubrey Beardsley were major sources, sometimes plagiarised directly as in *Big Brother & The Holding Co.* 1967. They also inspired sinuous bands of illegible words winding around pretty ladies, and off-centre compositions, with decorative elements included for their own sake, as in the poster by Stanley Mouse and Alton Kelley for *Miller Blues Band/Mother Earth* 1967.

The letters on rock posters in 1967–68 are all but unreadable. Elaborate lettering was a vital component of the overall design — in Wes Wilson's *Van Morrison* 1967 they form the image —

Wes Wilson *Van Morrison/The Daily Flash/Hair* 1967 lithograph

Robert Fried *The High Mass is coming in November* 1967 lithograph

Unknown artist after **Alphonse Mucha** *Big Brother & The Holding Co.* 1967 lithograph

Martin Sharp *Mister tambourine man* 1968 screenprint on foil paper

Stanley Mouse and **Alton Kelley** *Miller Blues Band/Mother Earth* 1967 lithograph

but also served a more important purpose. Oldies and straights couldn't decipher them. Even the hip entrepreneur Bill Graham didn't get the point entirely, according to Wilson who worked for him. His boss complained: 'Who cares about this lady in the drawing? They want to see the bands. You should have made the names much bigger.'[3]

According to Graham, who commissioned the works, artists were obscuring the issue. He considered that:

> the basic point of the poster is to transmit information, to communicate information about concerts. But I understood their desire, in this wonderful, childish, scheming way, to bury all the pertinent information underneath all the oozes and ebbs and flows and liquidy movement on the poster.[4]

In the sixties, posters changed their meaning. They had always been public advertisements, shown in the streets; now posters entered the private spaces of young people's bedrooms and living rooms. Large blow-ups taken from black and white photographs of movie stars (especially Humphrey Bogart, Jean Harlow and James Dean) suddenly became popular, closely followed by West Coast psychedelia. Posters were used for decoration, as a statement of lifestyle, and for staring at while stoned.

The Australian artist Martin Sharp, working in London from 1967 to 1969, is perhaps the most talented graphic artist of the time. His best-known image is the cover for Cream's album *Disraeli Gears* 1967. A poster of Bob Dylan, *Mister tambourine man* 1968, combines fantastically drawn lettering and decorations with photographs of the singer–songwriter, a hero of the counter culture. No surface is left untreated. Circles on circles form the famous halo of hair, and the sun and planets. Patterns and quotations stand inside other letters, even in the lens of Dylan's ever-present dark glasses ('Blowing in the mind'), the whole screenprinted in black and orange on gold foil. Sharp's wonderfully anarchic renderings are characterised by the artist's individual lettering, inflated like asymmetrical balloons, slanting positives against negatives, and strongly shadowed.

Sunshine superman 1968, Sharp's portrait of the British bard Donovan, superimposes the image over the writing, rather than integrating the two. Donovan is contained within a blue rectangle, the rest printed in black, and the disparate elements unified by a silver ground. Perhaps less successful than *Mister tambourine man* because less single-minded, the visual cacophony nevertheless evokes myriad pleasures.

In *Vincent* 1968, a homage to Van Gogh, Sharp refers to the famous work *Sunflowers* by collaging the painter's self-portraits among yellow and white flowers, and sunny yellow discs and rays. Van Gogh stands at his easel with a comic-strip bubble thought:

> I have a terrible lucidity at moments, when nature is so glorious. In those days I am hardly conscious of myself and the picture comes to me like in a dream …

The link between psychedelic drugs and creative inspiration is clear. Timothy Leary described the LSD experience as 'retinal orgasm'.

Underground heroes tended to be romantically lone males such as Van Gogh, Dylan or Hendrix. Cult novels had similar subjects, as in Jack Kerouac's fictionalised portrait of Neal Cassady in the Beat classic *On the Road* 1955, Ken Kesey's *One Flew over the Cuckoo's Nest* 1963 and Hermann Hesse's 'wolf of the steppes' who gave his name to a book and a rock group, *Steppenwolf*. They were dark figures who often had tragic ends, in life as in fiction.

There was a countervailing attraction to fairy-tales and children's characters such as Peter Pan, Alice in Wonderland and Winnie the Pooh. Most popular was the fantasy world of J.R.R. Tolkien's *Lord of the Rings* 1954–55, with its noble elves, doughty dwarves and worthy hobbits, runic alphabets, myths, and its quest for treasure and wisdom. Tolkien's was another world to visit, like the attraction to exotic places such as Morocco and Nepal. The perils of cultural tourism, in real places where real people lived, and the dubious morality of wholesale cultural appropriation, were not yet clear.

Vague mysticism was the flavour of the decade (now revived in the nineties). Hindu, Muslim and Buddhist faiths from India, the Middle East and Africa, from China, Japan and

Martin Sharp *Vincent* 1968 photolithograph

Unknown artist *Baltimore Steam Packet/Moby Grape/Only Alternatives and His Other Possibilities* 1967 lithograph

Victor Moscoso (**Paul Kagan**, photographer) *Youngbloods/The Other Half/ Mad River* 1967 lithograph

Southeast Asia, became fashionable in European and North American societies. Youth was seeking something more than the prosperity offered by the 'successful' materialism of industrial capitalism. The adoption of Zen sometimes implied nothing but disdain for Western institutions, rather than the reality of an arcane, disciplined system of Buddhist religious beliefs.

Christian churches were repudiated by most young people, who saw them as hypocritical, propping up the 'system'. The rationality of Western science was rejected also. Science and technology led inexorably to the atom bomb, to the machinery of death being used in Vietnam, and to pollution of the Earth, a concern which increased throughout the sixties.

Although some were interested only in the East — Tantric yoga, the Taoist *I-ching* [*The book of changes*], Sufism, or even all of them — the tradition of European mysticism was revived also. Astrology and the tarot had long been naturalised in the West from their Near Eastern roots, and the 'science' of telling the future was adopted as part of the ambient hippy culture. Nostradamus and other books from the Middle Ages such as herbals made old woodcuts familiar, and poster artists adopted them. The anonymous designer of *Baltimore Steam Packet/Moby Grape/Only Alternatives and His Other Possibilities* 1967 took the medieval woodcut rendering of a jester, added swirling letters and printed the whole in shades of purple and green.

Poster artists borrowed from contemporary high art styles as well. For his dazzling *Rolling Stones* 1967, Rich Charter used visual effects known from Op art and the popular deceptive optical 'puzzles' of M. C. Escher. A tone drop-out photograph of the group is made from concentric circles, printed in blue over strong, reverberating rays of orange and red. Uncertainties of perception are accentuated by the caption 'Rolling Stones' being printed back to front at the top and upside down at the bottom of the poster.

Like the expansion of spiritual possibilities, sexual liberation became a mass phenomenon only in the 1960s. The contraceptive pill was used widely from the start of the decade. It was the openness with which the rebels treated sex that was revolutionary and shocking to 'respectable' people. Monogamy and marriage implied possession and lack of freedom, the ultimate value of the time.

Drugs cast off sexual constraints as well as other social inhibitions. Victor Moscoso uses a photograph by Paul Kagan for the patterned silhouette of a pair of naked lovers in his dance concert poster for *Youngbloods/The Other Half/Mad River* 1967. Energy and joy are conveyed by the two dancing figures, covered and framed in stars and rainbow designs of orange, green, blue and pink.

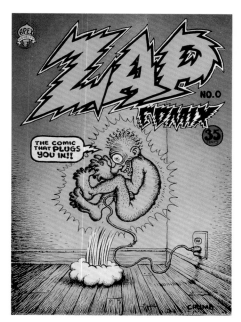  

R. Crumb *Zap Comix* No.0 October 1967, No.1 November 1967, No.2 1968 lithographs

Rich Charter *Rolling Stones* 1967 screenprint

Rick Griffin *The Who/Poco/The Bonzo Dog Band* 1969 lithograph

Unknown artist (**Paul Kagan**, photographer) *Peace sign c.*1968 lithograph

many comic strip conventions, but as the cover of *Zap* No. 1, November 1967, stated, 'Fair warning: For adult intellectuals only!' *Zap* No. 2, 1968, offered 'kozmic trooths' as well. His characters have sex, smoke dope and taunt authority. Fritz the Cat, a streetwise feline, displays all the cool (and sexism) of the time. Crumb's best-known work is perhaps his brilliant cover for Big Brother & the Holding Company's 1968 classic album, *Cheap Thrills*.

As the decade neared its end, more and more poster artists incorporated photographic elements into their designs. Bill Bractis printed a negative in blue and red for *Moby Grape/ Its a Beautiful Day/The Other Half/Tim Hardin/Jerry Abrams* 1969. The central image, a portrait head, is flanked by lettering that does not impinge into the picture. A head of wild hair, the 'Afro' fashionable for blacks and whites alike, masses its intricate filaments and segues into a halo. Lee Conklin engulfs a photograph of the Grateful Dead in dark red and orange flames in *Grateful Dead/Pentangle/Sir Douglas Quintet* 1969. Tongues of fire form skulls and faces, almost indistinguishable from the fiery letters spelling out its message.

In his poster for *Jefferson Airplane/Charlie Musselwhite/The Ceyleib People* 1968, John Van Hamersveld shows a new respect for other cultures. The artist frames his appropriated photograph of a native American with a border based on the traditional American Indian craft of beadwork. The lettering is incorporated into the patterns of tiny squares, so that it is nearly indecipherable. The photographer (Jerry Wainwright), not a designer, is credited on *Country Joe & the Fish/Pacific Gas & Electric* 1969. Modestly produced, printed in black and white, the work shows a naked woman in the lotus position, a flower in her lap.

The high-tech look of science fiction illustration, mainly identified with heavy metal and hard rock bands, is an alternative kind of mysticism. In his poster for *The Who/Poco/ The Bonzo Dog Band* 1969, Rick Griffin creates an almost threatening metaphor from the world of insects. A humanoid beetle squats under the butterfly-shaped headline 'The Who'. Lines like antennae creep up the poster, finally resolving into spiky lettering. The artist makes the colours reverberate by printing brilliant red over blue merging into magenta.

Perhaps it indicates the end of an era that the poster for Woodstock is indistinguishable from commercial art. Like the West Coast artists, Arnold Skolnick juxtaposes bold, opposing primary colours without intervening lines — but the result is static and conventional. Skolnick realises the motto of Woodstock, *3 days of peace & music* 1969, as the dove of peace perching on the neck of a guitar. The festival's importance has made the poster into an icon, ensuring its immortality.

Such explicit depictions of uninhibited sexuality would have been unthinkable in the puritanical United States even two years before. Book censorship was being challenged, and the Hayes film code was quietly discarded. A decorative poster, *Peace sign c.*1968, catches the moment: a photographic drop-out shows lovers having sex, printed in orange against a background mandala of purple and green paisley. It looks crude today, but the vulgarity is artistic rather than sexual. Upright citizens in every country were outraged by such public expressions of activity which they thought belonged only to the private sphere. 'Honesty' to some was 'obscenity' to others.

The counter culture claimed love as its territory. *Haight is love* proclaimed the poster, announcing San Francisco's 'summer of love' (1967) in the Haight-Ashbury district. When John Lennon and Yoko Ono married in 1969, they held a 'bed-in for peace' to protest against the Vietnam War. It was staged in the headquarters of the European counter culture, liberal Amsterdam (albeit in the luxurious surroundings of the local Hilton hotel). This was a kind of protest influenced by the most radical movement of modernism, Conceptual art.

Ono had been an avant-garde artist in Japan and the United States until she became Lennon's wife and musical partner. Their album, *Two Virgins* 1968, showed the famous couple full frontal naked on the cover, and a rear view on the back — possibly the first album sold with a compulsory covering bag. Is this only for shock value, or to break down barriers, or for liberation which would lead to global peace and the triumph of alternative values? What divided the mainstream from others, mainly the young, were fundamental differences of opinion about sexuality, drugs and especially the morality of the Vietnam War.

R. Crumb's funky comic strips, particularly *Zap Comix*, flaunted the hip values which seemed prevalent in the laid-back West Coast of the United States. Crumb continued

John Van Hamersveld *Jefferson Airplane/Charlie Musselwhite/The Ceyleib People* 1968 lithograph

Roy Lichtenstein *Brushstrokes* 1967 screenprint

new art met general incomprehension and dismay. Despite their personally radical political beliefs and rhetoric, it now seems that these artists had not come to grips with the anti-elitist climate of the time, nor to have engaged the new climate of mass culture. A lot of art was visually unappealing, stripped of aesthetic values.

There was a fundamental division between public and private culture, enunciated clearly for the first time in the late 1960s. A new, large, literate mass audience chose to watch TV and films, to read magazines and listen to the radio or go to pop concerts, rather than to read books, visit museums or attend classical music concerts.

High art had always assumed an educated, cultivated, even wealthy clientele, who bought objects — paintings, sculptures, prints, even photographs — for their own collections. The critics, and dealers too, ensured that museums acquired them. But the very nature of Post-object, Idea or Conceptual art, or *Arte povera* (Poor art), denied the possibility of purchase. How could you buy a concept? A landscape? A wrapped public building? Crowds? Spontaneity?

It is one of the contradictions at this time that the democratic ideals of artists meant that they would not be able to make a living from their work. In the revolutionary situation of 1968, it seemed that capitalist structures such as the art market would be broken down. Public commissions, or a state wage for artists, might change the old ways.

But the capitalist system and the art market won in the end. Even the purist Conceptual artists ended up selling the documentation of their works in order to finance new projects. Art and Language ran out of enthusiasts, and Christo sold plans, drawings and photographs of his public projects. Most artists stayed within the gallery system, with hot-shot dealers publicising their work, marketing an image to avant-garde art magazines, collectors and museums. Some, like Hans Haacke, attempted to challenge the system from within.

Political art was very difficult for museums to swallow. When it challenged their own values, it became impossible. The issue was highlighted with the publication of an Art Workers Coalition poster about the Vietnam War, originally a co-production with the Museum of Modern Art, New York. The unthinkable reality of Americans slaughtering civilians in Vietnam, revealed by the *New York Times* in 1969, was documented with graphic colour photographs and film. The confrontational and distressing poster *Q. And babies? A. And babies.* 1969 was taken from Ronald Haeberle's colour photograph of the My Lai massacre in 1968. The horror was too much for the museum's trustees, who took refuge in an old defence: the inalienable separation of art from politics.

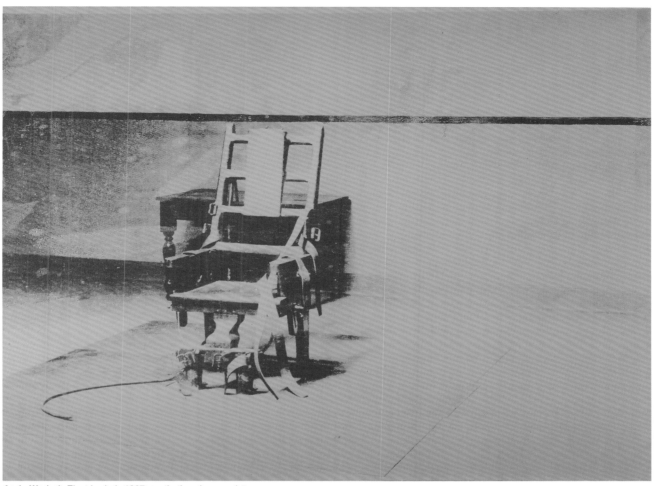

Andy Warhol *Electric chair* 1967 synthetic polymer paint on canvas

Art Workers Coalition (**Ronald Haeberle**, photographer) *Q. And babies? A. And babies.* 1969 photolithograph

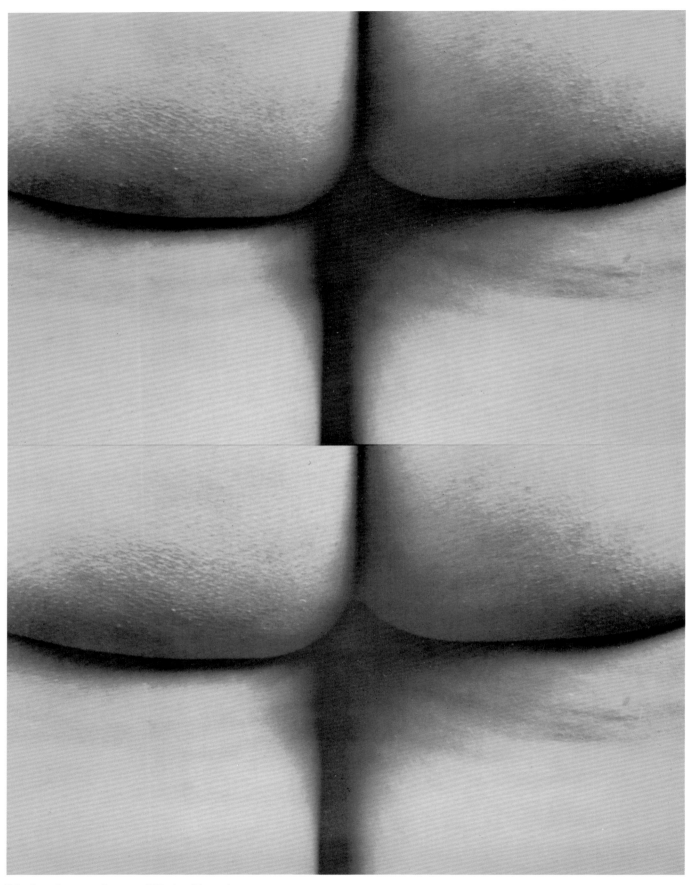

Yoko Ono *Bottoms* wallpaper *c.*1968 photolithographs

40

1967
Walter Lowenfels *Where is Vietnam?*
American Poets Respond /
Marshall McLuhan and Quentin Fiore
The Medium Is the Massage
1968
Eldridge Cleaver *Soul on Ice* /
Joan Didion *Slouching Towards
Bethlehem* / Free (Abbie Hoffman)
Revolution For the Hell of It / Timothy
Leary *The Politics of Ecstasy* /
Norman Mailer *Armies of the Night* /
Desmond Morris *The Naked Ape* /
Peter Nichols *A Day in the Death of
Joe Egg* / Joe Orton *Loot* / John Updike
Couples / Gore Vidal *Myra Breckinridge* /
Tom Wolfe *The Electric Kool-aid Acid Test*
1969
Jerry Farber *The Student as Nigger* /
Abbie Hoffman *Woodstock Nation:
A Talk-rock Album* / Theodore Roszak
The Making of a Counter Culture /
Jerry Rubin *Do It!*

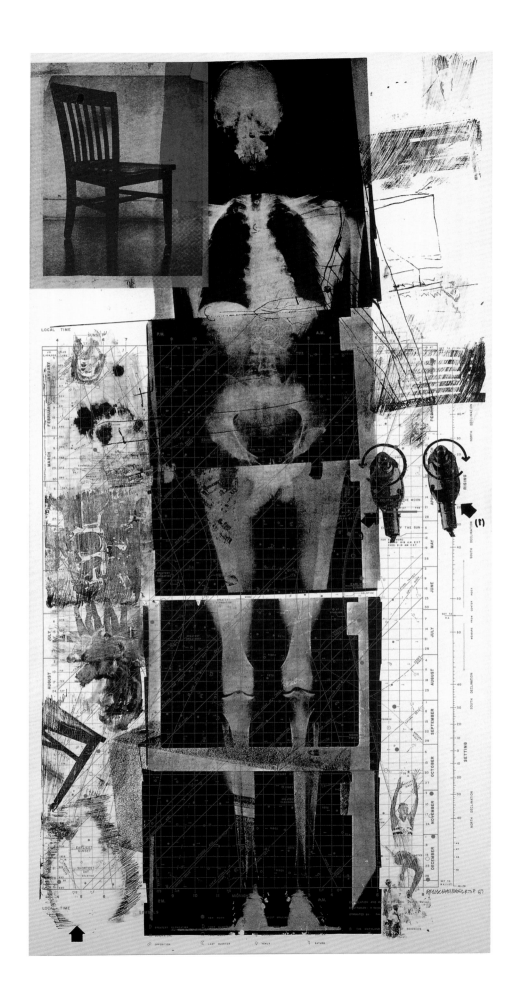

42

Professors you are old, and so is your culture

graffiti, Paris, May '68

The citadel of the avant-garde

High art took new forms. In 1968 Mel Ramsden completed his *Guarantee painting*. It consisted of a small white canvas, accompanied by a certificate of authenticity which guaranteed the (invisible) contents. In September that year Walter de Maria filled three rooms of the Galerie Heiner Friedrich in Munich with a metre of dirt. In New York, Seth Siegelaub published *Carl Andre, Robert Barry, Douglas Huebler, Joseph Kosuth, Sol LeWitt, Robert Morris, Lawrence Weiner* 1968: the catalogue was the exhibition.

It is cliché that art reflects life. One would expect some sort of accord between art and the culture from which it derives, yet much of the cool, ironic and self-referential art of the late sixties appears isolated from the heated politics, the idealism and concern for the natural, the emotional, 'do your own thing' and 'let it all hang out' attitudes by which the sixties are characterised.

The social and political crisis of the late 1960s was matched by equivalent challenges within the art world, and by radical transformations in the advanced art of the time. While modern art had always held itself aloof from local politics, the convulsions of the late sixties were to make an impact even on this intellectual island. The social developments and political consequences of the period were not manifested directly in its art, though of course these were part of the experience of the artists.

Artistic revolution followed a similar schedule to social revolution, but with a different itinerary. The crisis in art was expressed almost exclusively within the discipline. The relevance of the existing models of art practice was questioned, as was the capacity of art to maintain its connections with society. Artistic evolution in the sixties on one hand concerned itself with problems and issues intrinsic to itself, and on the other searched for meanings outside art.

Robert Rauschenberg *Booster* from *Booster and seven studies* 1967
colour lithograph, screenprint

The two branches of this evolution began to pull in opposite directions, creating in 1968 a powerful pressure and a number of inventive strategies to resolve the tension.

Pop: romancing the public
There seems to be a direct relationship between the Pop art spawned in the late fifties and early sixties and its own era. Consumer culture is represented and critiqued in all its self-congratulatory egalitarianism. Pop artists reflected the optimism of mainstream prosperity through images of film stars and comic-book characters, soup cans and hamburgers, shoes, chairs and the utensils of everyday existence.

Though cool in style, Pop art was appreciably public, and calculatedly theatrical. It adopted commercial means of image-making, such as screenprinting and photography, and such techniques of mass advertising as persuasive colour combinations, bold presentations, iconic compositions and direct messages.

Proto-pop artist Robert Rauschenberg was one of the first to borrow from mass media. Typically, his works collaged images from the newspapers, from journals of art, medicine or business, with pictures taken from junk mail catalogues or television. In the human-scale print *Booster* 1967, the logic of these connections is not immediately apparent: there is no simple narrative. Rauschenberg's combinations echo the random nature of the newspaper's front page or the varied content of television. His compositions of unrelated subject matter are unified only by the medium itself — here lithography with screenprinting.

The flood of mediated images was unprecedented in the 1960s. This was the first generation to be brought up on a regular diet of television. It was the age when advances in printing made publications cheap, and colour reproductions were increasingly available, in everything from art magazines to women's journals. The photographs in *Booster* — the artist's own x-rayed skeleton, a chair, electric drills, a

Toaster

New, practical, outstanding, this print was made possible by a number of fresh ideas. The proof of the excellence of the toaster that inspired this work of art has been supplied by the results of severe endurance tests recently performed. The appliance was kept working for a total of 1458.3 hours (not counting brief periods for cooling). This was the time taken to toast 50 000 slices of bread. That is a pile of bread well over a quarter of a mile high.
Just how outstanding the design is can be proved by the fact that it has been included among the most attractive objects for everyday use exhibited at the New York Museum of Modern Art – the only automatic toaster in the world to achieve this honour.
White bread, black bread or even rye bread? Ask your friends and neighbours and they will tell you that toast is a first-class delicacy. It tastes good and has never been the cause of anyone losing their driving licence. It keeps you fit and your body needs it.

Printed on Saunders plain mould special printing s/o demi 80.5 lb/500 (complete with Marlerfilm and Marlerflex ink and applied metallized silver polyester) in an edition of 75.
Dimensions 25'' wide, 35'' high, image area 23'' square.

Richard Hamilton *Toaster* 1967 lithograph, screenprint, metallised polymer film

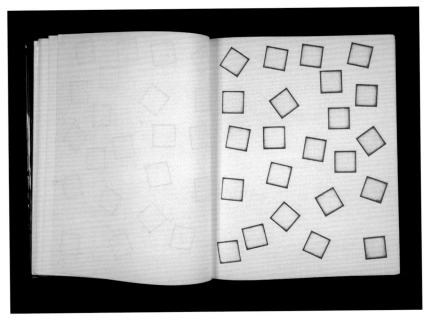

Carl Andre Page from *Carl Andre, Robert Barry, Douglas Huebler, Joseph Kosuth, Sol LeWitt, Robert Morris, Lawrence Weiner* 1968 photocopy

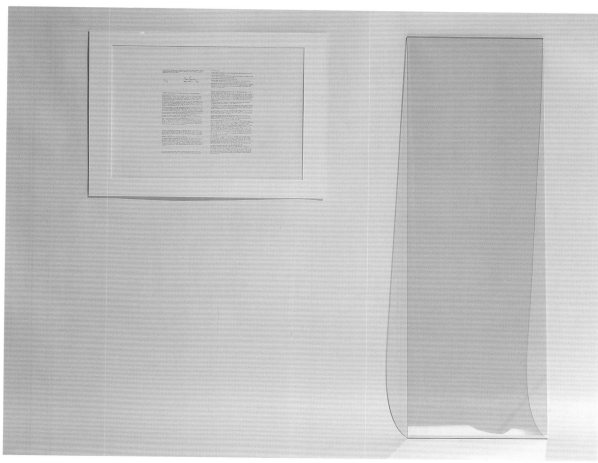

Ian Burn *Undeclared glass* 1967 letterpress, glass

celestial map — document the varied world of images in Rauschenberg's milieu.

The combinations reflect confidence in scientific achievement and American aspirations. Speaking of Rauschenberg's work in a lecture given at New York's Museum of Modern Art in 1968, Leo Steinberg described the use of cheek-by-jowl images from mass media as 'the most radical shift in the subject matter of art, the shift from nature to culture'.[5]

Richard Larter, who arrived in Australia from the United Kingdom in 1962, also constructs his paintings with a montage of found images from common source material. In spite of their deliberate 'crudeness', Larter's images seem less raw than the American's. Perhaps this is because they are described with paint — photographs transferred onto the canvas via another medium. The provocative pairing of nudes and political figures (and their tools) in Larter's *Big time easy mix* 1967 is designed to shock with its swinging modern morality.

'Obscenity', wrote Herbert Marcuse in 1968,

> is a moral concept in the verbal arsenal of the Establishment, which abuses the term by applying it, not to expressions of its own morality but to those of another. Obscene is not the picture of a naked woman who exposes her pubic hair but that of a fully clad general who exposes his medals rewarded in a war of aggression ...[6]

Marcuse argued that change does not come about solely by altering political institutions, but through the transformation of culture. A contemporary slogan, 'the personal is political', marks a new attitude that ties personal behaviour to social responsibility.

Larter is up to date with his politics, but the all but expressionist technique looks curiously old-fashioned by now. The heated content and comment go against the conventional cool of the 'laid back' era, and seem obstinately English. Larter refers to the original printed source through painterly marks and hatching, echoing the printing process, but without relinquishing the high-art status of painting.

Richard Larter *Big time easy mix* 1969 synthetic polymer paint on composition board

Roy Lichtenstein makes no such concessions with his technically slick screenprint *Brushstrokes* 1967, a witty comment on the trade between fine and commercial art. And returning the favour, a legion of ad-agency art directors took elements of Pop art to smarten up and decorate their trendy advertisements.

The confusion of high and low art forms did much to undermine the idea of an avant-garde. This shift in status, while it began in the early sixties, reached an all-time high in 1968. It was coupled with an equivalent confusion of social values. Larter was not alone in his use of soft-core pornography in art. The post-Pill sexual revolution had successfully challenged conventional morality. Regular exhibitions of erotic art provided a chance to gauge

acceptance of newly public sexuality. This varied, in art as much as in cinema and on the stage, where nudity became commonplace.

Allen Jones in his *Life class* 1968 poses the new woman as liberated in her sexuality. Each image is, in fact, a composite made from two halves, of the woman divided at the waist. In Jones's lithographs these are interchangeable, allowing him, the artist and ultimately the owner of the portfolio, to create a succession of new models. His creatures are victims of fashion, teased by their creator into alluring form-fitting outfits that defy anatomy. Liberation ostensibly offered women (and men) the opportunity to fulfil themselves, but, in practice, became a device to sell books, magazines, films and lithographs.

Allen Jones from *Life class* 1968 lithographs, photolithographs

48

It is forbidden to forbid -
by decree 10 May 1968

graffiti, Paris, May '68

Minimal art

Cool, aloof, and severely abstract, Minimal art seemed a rock in a shifting landscape. It was uncompromising, apparently offering no point of engagement to any but the cadre most involved with the fine arts. Perhaps there is no more than coincidence in the uncanny resemblance between the black monolith that appeared in the opening scenes of *2001: A Space Odyssey*, the 1968 film by Stanley Kubrick, and a typical work of contemporary sculpture on display in any number of New York galleries at the time. Popular opinion certainly perceived that such a form was an alien artefact, sophisticated but impenetrable.

Minimal art was not immune from tradition, however. It is the legitimate heir to American modernism, linked to Abstract Expressionism through Colour-field painting in the late fifties, as practised by Kenneth Noland, Ellsworth Kelly, Morris Louis and Jules Olitski. Increasingly geometric, Colour-field painters accepted that the Cubist grid was the foundation of Abstract Expressionism, and they played large planes of colour across the canvas.

Artists chose to separate their art from the emotional *angst* of the previous generation. They favoured purely formal relationships, striving to empty all pictorial content from abstraction. In distancing themselves from Abstract Expressionist artists, they rejected individualism and the 'autograph touch' in an effort to achieve objective clarity. They initiated a dominant tendency of the sixties, the movement to reductivism, which eventually made the art object itself superfluous.

Colour-field artists banished modelling and tone from paintings and colour from sculpture. According to Clement Greenberg, the prime quality of painting was its flatness, due in part to the shape of the support and to the properties of pigment. For sculpture, it was three-dimensionality. Such paintings were often characterised by flat uninflected areas of colour in abstract and generally austere designs. Colour, treated as areas of paint, not as illusionistic surface, was sharply bordered, giving the sobriquet 'hard edge' to these works.

For working artists and their audience in 1968 New York, there was no single dominating tendency, but rather a salad of styles: Colour-field painting co-existed with Pop art, Op art with Minimal art, the older generation of the New York School and their followers with the perennial army of realists. Australia on the other hand lacked the audience to support such diversity, and only two main camps existed. An expressionistic and figurative school dominated Melbourne, led by the artists of the Antipodean group (formed in 1959) as the intellectual core for broadcasting national themes. Sydney vanguard artists, on the other hand, were cautiously international, and championed an expressionistic abstraction informed by European *Tachisme*.

Australians were reasonably well informed of overseas developments through exhibitions brought to major cities, by journals and by overseas travel. Sydney hosted an exhibition of young British artists in 1964 that included Pop works by David Hockney and Richard Smith. The American vanguard was represented in The Michener Collection of American Art, shown the same year. Of greater importance was the exhibition *Two Decades of American Painting*, shown in Melbourne and Sydney in 1967. It confirmed the importance of American influence on Australian culture, and endorsed the hard-edged style of Colour-field painting to the locals.

The native expressionism of the Antipodean artists was overwhelmed by the self-evident importance of modernity and internationalism in the American work: 'Once again Melbourne has been dragged screaming into the twentieth century' trumpeted the Melbourne *Age*'s art critic Patrick McCaughey.[7]

Paul Partos *Yellow screen with yellow* and *Black screen* 1968
painted nylon and wood

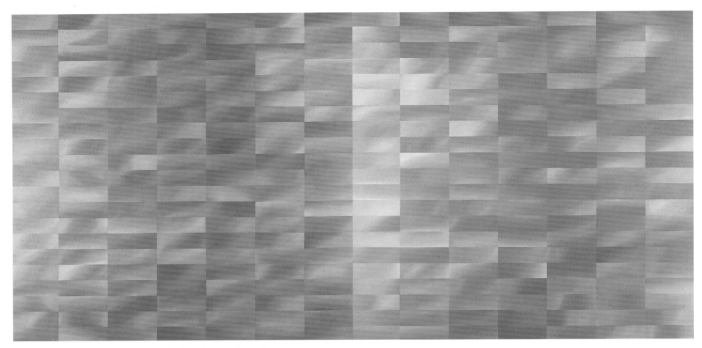

Dale Hickey *Atlantis wall* 1969 synthetic polymer paint on two canvases

The following year, to mark the reopening of the National Gallery of Victoria and to inform Australia that the year 1968 was indeed part of the twentieth century, an exhibition *The Field* was mounted to show the work of Australian artists using the new 'hard-edge' style.

While critics then, and since, have made much of the imposition of the 'international' style on local experimentation, it was a case of trying to shut the stable door. Many of the artists in *The Field* had worked abroad in any case, and few would not have seen the imported exhibitions or illustrations in art journals. Artists also bring their own history into their work and offer their own interpretation of styles. Robert Rooney and Dale Hickey, for example, had been figurative artists in the early sixties: the abstract works they produced during 1968 derived from personal observation.

Both Hickey's *Atlantis wall* 1969 and Rooney's *Kind-hearted kitchen garden II* 1967, unlike the Americans' works, somehow never sever connections with reality. They project as much sensory as cerebral information. *Wall II* 1968–69 by Janet Dawson flirts with this distinction between the abstract and the figurative. Her skewed grid of grey panels pushes out of the picture plane in a disconcertingly architectural way. Blushes of pink in the grey paint subtly reinforce this seeming projection, as does the combination of ochre and black stripes in the gridding. A set of lighter panels promotes the feeling of sun-bleached masonry, without relinquishing the reality that this is paint on a flat surface.

Gunter Christmann ostensibly observes the protocols of Greenbergian theory in his stripped forms of the late sixties. His painting, however, is not concerned only with geometry or with purely formalist values. *Big black* 1969 shows other leanings in the textured paintwork and the optical play of colour on the retina.

In *The Field* exhibition of 1968 Robert Hunter presented works of dazzling purity, in thought and in deed. His monochrome paintings were notable for their self-sufficiency and sophistication, surprising from an artist in his early twenties. Hunter combined a non-colour (white) with a transparent composition (a grid of regularly placed circles) indicated by the merest inflection on the paint surface. *Untitled* 1968 tested theoretical as well as visual acuity.

The subtle beauty of Hunter's canvas is beyond the sensitivity of film emulsion, and the painting could not be reproduced in *The Field* catalogue. It hangs on the threshold of perception. In 1917–18, after a startling decade of innovation, Kazimir Malevich had brought his art to a climax with his white-on-white paintings. Could painting progress beyond this point? Hunter and his generation created the same dilemma a second time.

In 1968 it was very important to be true to material. In a sense, the 'purity of medium' gave an advantage to sculpture. Painting had colour to play with, but this had to be flat and unmodulated. The shape of the canvas could be varied, but after many permutations it was realised that the external shape worked best when it reiterated the internal elements in the composition, as in the early work of Frank Stella, or as seen in Margaret Worth's undulating shaped canvas, *Samsara 17* 1969. Eventually, however, the outcome was too easy to predict.

If painting had to deny the illusion of the third dimension, it was possible to alter the canvas itself to project into space. In Jo Baer's *Untitled (Vertical flanking diptych — red)* 1966–74 (painted 1967), bands of colour echo the frame shape, while the two panels exert a strong physical presence. In the Summer 1967 issue of *Artforum* Robert Morris criticised painting's inherent and incorrigible illusionism. In response,

Gunter Christmann *Big black* 1969 synthetic polymer paint on canvas

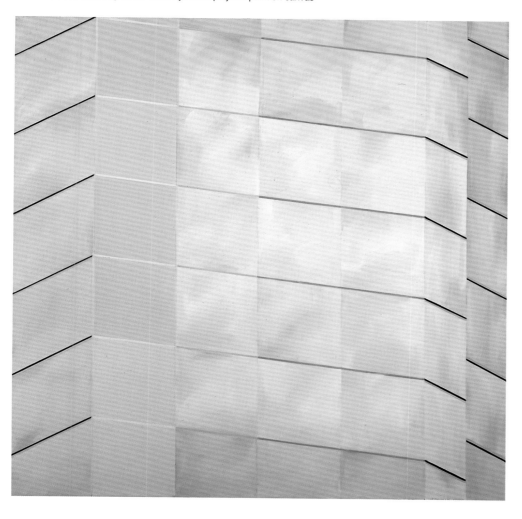

Janet Dawson *Wall II* 1968–69
synthetic polymer paint on canvas

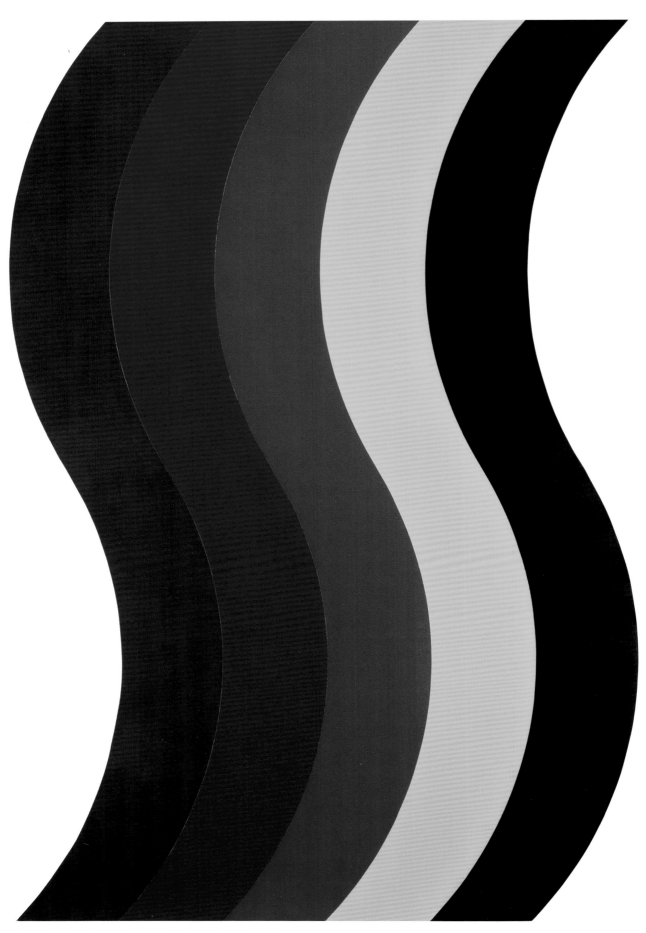

Margaret Worth *Samsara 17* 1969 synthetic polymer paint on plywood

Jo Baer asserted the primacy of painting as a radical art form. Nevertheless, in a number of paintings made towards the end of 1967 and in 1968, Baer felt the need to accentuate the object status of her paintings and started to extend the painted surface over the edges of the canvas.

The sides of the stretcher could be widened until the painting stood proud of the wall as an object, or alternatively it could be broken into components to create a low relief. Michael Johnson explores this path in his *Frontal red* 1969. The work is built with several canvases, each a pure colour. The play of tones between the separate units encourages spatial readings, although the integrity of the medium is maintained.

Paul Partos, in his two works, *Yellow screen with yellow* 1968 and *Black screen* 1968–69, has adopted a more radical approach. The 'proud' canvas has been taken off the wall completely, to stand upright in space. Partos replaces the canvas with nylon mesh and applies colour with a spray gun. The superimposition and transparency of the mesh effects moiré patterns, articulating the surface of the works. *Black screen* appears as a slice of hazy atmosphere transposed to the gallery floor. The works nonetheless lack the substance of sculpture, and the issues of colour and

surface dealt with are those of painting. Partos's solution to the crisis in art produces neither sculpture nor painting, but a curious hybrid, a seductive conflation of genres.

If painting aspired to the qualities of sculpture, then so too did sculpture begin to resemble painting. Sculptor Donald Judd preferred not to call his work sculpture. He expressed a desire to create work that existed 'between sculpture and painting'. Nigel Lendon was clearly influenced by the example of contemporary painting in *Untitled floor structure 1969–1* 1969, but also by recent developments in Minimal art. His slab-like sculpture lies on the floor like a fallen painting.

Lendon avoids the need for a base, just as a painting on a wall would. His licorice-allsort layers of orange, lavender, red and pale blue-grey suggest a stack of modular units, each half sculpture, half painting. In colonising the floor Lendon sculpturally activates the space inhabited by the work with something decidedly concrete and literal. His use of the floor as support approaches a painter's use of 'ground' in a painting. This (coupled with his use of colour and sense of illusion) puts his work, like so many other sculptures of the period, directly in competition with painting.

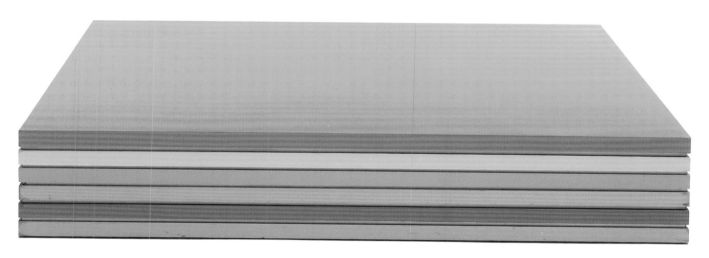

Nigel Lendon *Untitled floor structure 1969–1* 1969 painted wood

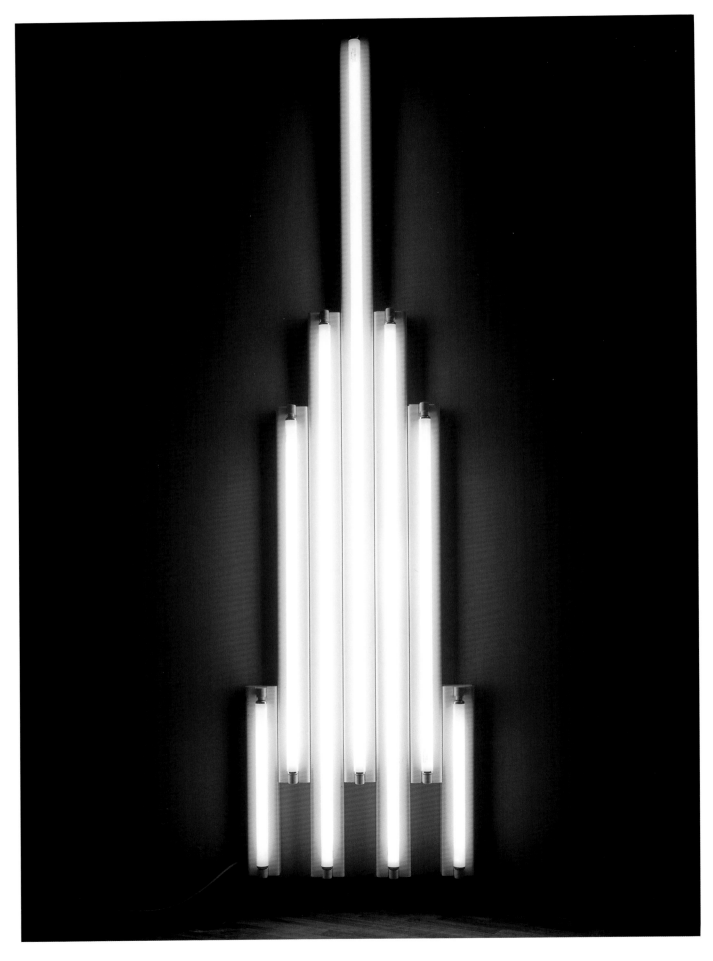

Difficult things can be achieved. The impossible takes a little longer.

graffiti after Santayana, Paris, May '68

The ascendancy of sculpture

Minimal art, the dominant art form in the late sixties, was almost exclusively concerned with sculpture. Sculpture, like painting, was restricted by modernist theory. In the credo of 'truth to materials', it had the advantage that it could be made of many substances, each with different properties to determine the final form.

Sculptors began to experiment with a range of possibilities traditional and new, those materials without an artistic history. Artists used established materials — glass, wood, wax, steel, plexiglass — but also a variety of factory-produced or natural additions to the traditional repertoire: neon tubing, plywood, resin and fibreglass, polyurethane, aluminium, felt, rubber, rock and earth, for example.

Artists maintained the integrity of industrial materials by retaining prefabricated proportions in their work. As these sizes tended to be based on their portability by the average worker, the resultant works of art are held to human proportions. Such objects were, for the most part, constructed and viewed within architectural settings.

Robert Morris established himself as one of the earliest exponents of what was to be called Minimal art with his first solo exhibitions in New York at the Green Gallery. There he exhibited large, grey painted, plywood geometric forms intended to have limited visual appeal. These works were placed on the floor of the gallery, suspended from the roof, or across corners. The 'units' (they bore a relationship to one another) had no pedestals, were austere to the point of being aggressively abstract, and were plainly sculpture — architectural, yet distinct from architecture.

Like architecture, Morris's sculpture defines itself in relation to the viewer, while channelling the audience's interaction. Two of these early sculptures (*Cloud* and *Slab* 1962) are effectively the same work, but difference in their placement alters the

perception of each work, heightening our engagement with the geometry of the surrounding space. Volume and mass remain primary sculptural concerns, but what is announced is the simplicity, clarity and unprecedented degree of anti-illusionism.

Other 'neutral' objects by other artists associated with Minimalism — Sol LeWitt, Donald Judd, Carl Andre, to name the best known — appeared to extend the currency of formalism. But conservative critics such as Clement Greenberg were quick to spot apostasy, describing Minimalism, along with Assemblage, Pop, Environment, Op, Kinetic and Erotic, as 'Novelty Art'.[8] Michael Fried recognised that the interaction between the object and the viewer was theatrical, and asserted that 'theatre is now the negation of art'.[9] Minimalism was in fact decidedly anti-formalist.

Sol LeWitt used the grid as his primary motif, effectively neutralising composition, the rationale for formalism. *Cubic modular piece No 3* 1968 can be as authoritative as a barred gate or as passive as office furniture. In common with many contemporary sculptures it can be taken in at a glance: there is order and clarity in its machine-like logic. Once the viewer's angle of inspection changes, the classical veneer gives way to criss-crossing members, diagonal shadows and gothic detail and complexity.

LeWitt employed repetition, itself a variation of the grid. When this was coupled with the industrial materials used, Minimal sculpture began to look like a comment on twentieth-century production. The fact that most of the artists had their sculptures fabricated by others compounded this notion. It did not alter the aesthetic qualities of the work in any way. Instead, the unique authority of the artist was undermined, often consciously. As the name suggests, *Cubic modular piece No 3* is the third in a series of related works, each a development of the grid structure. The permutations deriving from a systemic approach reintroduced the element of chance into art.

Dan Flavin *monument to V. Tatlin* 1966–69 fluorescent tubes

Claes Oldenburg *Miniature soft drum set* 1969 printed canvas, rope, wood and wooden box

Robert Morris's *Untitled* 1969 responds to chance each time it is set up. The felt bellies or pulls taut to effect a number of configurations, depending on the fall of the fabric. With its baroque curves and flounces, *Untitled* appears an unlikely product of Minimalism, although the grey felt has the right industrial connections and a familiar grimness.

Morris began using felt in 1967, slitting rectangles of the fabric into various configurations, much as LeWitt worked out permutations for his geometrical structures. The work was made from a long rectangle scored with eleven perpendicular cuts just stopping short of the edges of the fabric. Drawn as a diagram, *Untitled* would look similar to a page from Robert Jacks's book *1–12* 1969. In a harder material than felt, this would be orthodox Minimalism, but there is an unheard-of sensuousness here.

Robert Jacks made two drawings in 1969 that break the surface plane. *Rubber* and *Paper* rely on the same simple device that underpins Morris's felt: a series of regular cuts into a flat sheet (rubber or paper) with the knowledge that the material will respond with new forms. Cross-cuts determine that *Rubber* will be punctured with a grid of beaked holes, drawing attention to the flexibility of the membrane. Cut and curled, the low relief of *Paper* is equally a product of its constituent material. From such plain, unpromising resources, Jacks educes a surprising and satisfying harmony.

Claes Oldenburg showed with his surrealist-inspired 'soft sculpture' of the early sixties that sculpture could be made from pliable materials such as fabric or the new vinyl plastic sheeting (also used in the manufacture of inflatable furniture at this time). He made unfamiliar the prosaic domesticity of the light-switch, the hamburger or the toilet. Even drums, an icon in the age of rock music, were not immune. In his *Miniature soft drum set* 1969, sound is transformed into another, more ambiguous, idiom. And what Oldenburg had done to everyday things, Morris did to the square or cube by rendering it in compliant materials.

While the sixties were relaxing the rigid conceptions of what sculpture could or should be, there was a parallel relaxation of social mores in an attempt to get to the truth of things, to be natural. Informality seemed to extend itself into the

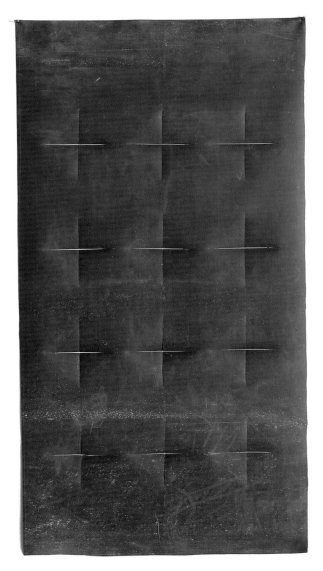

Robert Jacks *Rubber* 1969 cut rubber

arts as it did into all areas of society, responding to the changing mood of the sixties.

What had altered in the arts was a concern with the properties of the material itself. The felt in Morris's *Untitled* does not aspire to another condition, in the way that marble or bronze substitutes for flesh in traditional sculpture. Nor does his chosen medium take on symbolic attributes, as does Joseph Beuys's felt, standing for warmth and insulation. LeWitt's sculpture could be made of anything as it was a pure abstract creation, but Morris's chosen material is intrinsic to the form of the sculpture.

Still honouring formal relationships and the 'truth to material' ethic, sculptors saw the manipulation of that material as vital. This became known as 'process art', the creation of art by fusing its inherent qualities with the activity that creates it. Ian Burn's *Xerox book* 1968 is a classic example of this kind of art. Burn copied a white sheet of paper in a photocopier,

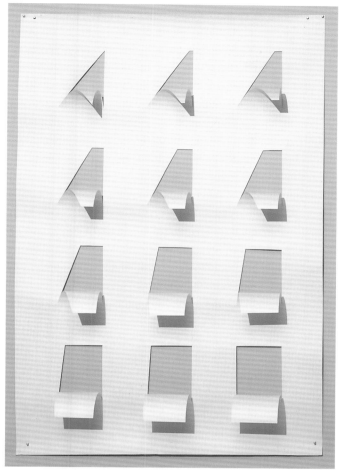

Robert Jacks *Paper* 1969 cut paper

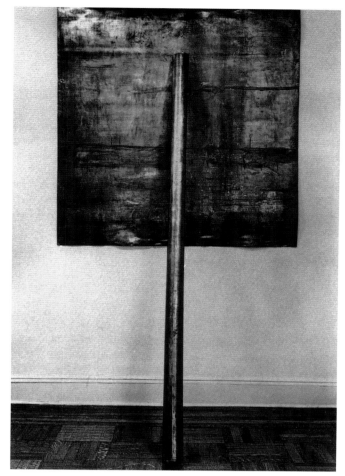

Richard Serra *Prop* 1968 lead

then copied the sheet that was produced, copying and recopying. The sheets, initially blank, were soon marked by the machine, and incorporated into the work in a paradigm of production and a partnership between artist and machine. There is directness and honesty in this approach, a relevance achieved by involving modernism with real materials and real processes. In repudiating composition by incorporating chance, or neutralising it with regular, geometric arrangements, artists discarded the values of formalism.

Contingent 1969 by Eva Hesse likewise assailed the idea of an art dependent on formal relationships. In common with the work of Minimal sculptors, hers is based on the repetition of units, but every part is different. Each unit, a hybrid of fibreglass and latex, is crinkled, organic, visceral, vulnerable — emotive forms rather than cool mathematical models. As architecture is the referent for Minimalists, so for Hesse it is the body.

It seemed as though the brave forms of the early part of the decade were sagging and withering with the burden of new references. *Contingent*, like Morris's *Untitled*, is sculptural in its response to gravity, to mass and form, but likewise ambiguous regarding the genre itself. Hesse retains a latent pictorialism. She indicated that the first panels could have hung on the wall as easily as Morris's work. Hesse tended to

use cheap, easily available materials, and techniques associated with women's activities — stitching and wrapping — to expand the vocabulary of artmaking.

Like Morris's *Untitled* and Hesse's *Contingent*, Richard Serra's *Prop* 1968 is located equivocally somewhere between wall and floor. *Prop* is made from two sheets of lead, the first held against the wall by the second, rolled to form a prop. Serra's work illustrates the temperament of the metal itself, both hard and soft. It shows his new way of approaching materials. 'I wrote down a list of transitive verbs', Serra said, 'to split, to splash, to spread, to roll, to heap ... and applied the infinitives.'[10]

Morris organised an exhibition, *9 at Castelli*, in December 1968 in which this work appeared along with those of Hesse, Bruce Nauman and others, a show which revealed a shift in art. In his polemical article 'Anti form', Morris stated:

Recently, materials other than rigid industrial ones have begun to show up ... A direct investigation of the properties of these materials is in progress. This involves a reconsideration of the use of tools in relation to the material.

Robert Morris *Untitled* 1969 felt

In some cases these investigations move from the making of things to the making of material itself. Sometimes a direct manipulation of a given material without the use of any tool is made. In these cases considerations of gravity become as important as those of space.[11]

Dan Flavin's sculpture *monument to V. Tatlin* 1966–69 utilises store-bought light fittings placed together in calculated variations. There is no further intervention by the artist, although this was not new. Much of the sculpture made by Morris, LeWitt, Donald Judd and others was fabricated to instructions provided by the artists, in the same way that an architect would provide plans for builders to carry out. The sculpture, if it is such, is the light itself and the area it defines. The work is ephemeral to the degree that it actually disappears the moment that the power is switched off.

Eva Hesse *Contingent* 1969 cheesecloth, latex, fibreglass

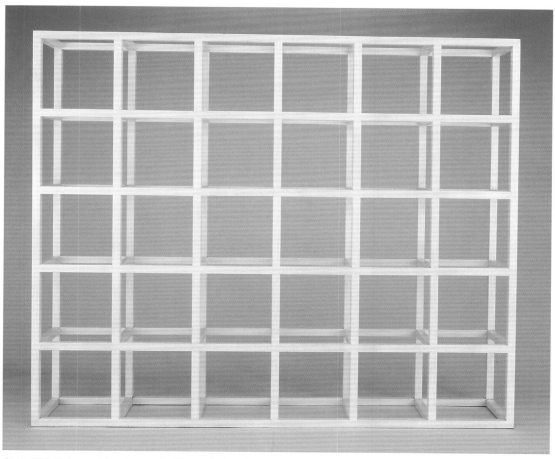

Sol LeWitt *Cubic modular piece no. 3* 1968 synthetic polymer paint on steel

When people notice they're bored, they stop being bored

graffiti, Paris, May '68

Into the ether

Like other forms of late sixties' art, *monument to V. Tatlin* is dependent on its setting — the museum or gallery — in order to be received as art. The 'ready-made' aspect of Flavin's work pays tribute to veteran artist Marcel Duchamp (who died in 1968). Duchamp announced in 1914 the primacy of *the idea* over the visual appearance of the art work. He named ordinary objects, a bottle rack or a hat rack, as art. Sol LeWitt confirmed that the idea is more important than the visual result, and that 'the idea becomes the machine that makes the art'.[12]

Assuming an art that was entirely an intellectual construction, Duchamp freed art from its technical roots. The idea of the 'ready-made' significantly expanded the subject matter of art to virtually anything, and implied that anyone could be an artist. Duchamp's ideas were discussed seriously in the sixties when the concept of democratising art was fashionable. Warhol had already scandalised and seduced with his *Brillo boxes*. Flavin's lights were intrinsically beautiful. What could go wrong?

Once it is accepted that physical form is secondary to the idea, it is only a matter of time before the object becomes unnecessary. Mel Ramsden draws attention to the unequal partnership between idea and physical realisation in his *Guarantee painting* 1967–68. The work consists of a small white canvas and a large certificate which guarantees the content of the painting, in this case an unseen circle of specified dimensions.

Ramsden's work pokes fun at the opacity of Minimal art and its reliance on theory, not without some irony. The catalogue for *The Field* exhibition carried details of Robert Hunter's painting *Untitled* 1968, but no illustration. It is imperative that the work be seen first hand. The canvas in Ramsden's *Guarantee painting* teeters on the edge of redundancy; it becomes a slave to the printed text.

Bruce Nauman *Self-portrait as a fountain* 1967 from *Eleven color photographs* 1966/67–1970 type C photograph

Ian Burn takes this relationship to an extreme in his sculpture *Undeclared glass* 1967, in which a printed screed on the wall accompanies several sheets of glass. They lean against the wall, casually, as if left there absent-mindedly by a builder or cleaner. Indeed there is nothing special about them. Burn specifies only that the work be installed with more than one sheet of glass, presumably so that it attains greater visibility, at the same time retaining a ghostly presence.

The document on the wall presents a densely argued thesis that art is an analytical proposition. It concludes with the notion that

> To describe the sheets of glass in any physical detail, or in terms of *use* as 'glass', is not after all to describe them as a work of art. To describe them as [a] work of art is, in essence, to make a statement that it is the case.

Burn's complex philosophical treatise asserts that art is only recognised culturally, through its contexts. The glass is offered as an example, just as a mathematician teaching algebra might choose to illustrate an equation with 'apples' or 'x'. The words are crucial, while the object is not.

Conceptual art, as it came to be known, could consist entirely of the 'idea' in a written form. The journal *Art — Language* (which numbers Mel Ramsden, Terry Atkinson, David Bainbridge, Sol LeWitt and Joseph Kosuth among its contributors) produced torrents of dense philosophical research into the nature of art. Aiming to promote greater understanding, the rarefied arguments in the journal were understood by fewer and fewer people. One of the paradoxes of Conceptual art was its ambition to clarify, although its propensity was to mystify.

'The true artist helps the world', Bruce Nauman stated in his neon *Window or wall sign* 1967, 'by revealing mystic truths.' Nauman's neon spiral puns the idea of 'illumination', and admits the mischief of circular argument. His plaintive advertisement for art is tinged with longing for an innocence before science equated facts with truth. In the Information Age, art might be relevant if artists only dealt in facts.

Mel Ramsden *Guarantee painting* 1967–68 oil on canvas with a gelatin silver photograph

Douglas Huebler *Location piece no. 2 July 1969* 1970 photolithographs

In an exercise worthy of a supercomputer, the artist Roman Opalka chose to paint every number from one to infinity. He started in Warsaw in 1965 and is still counting. Although Opalka has made numerous paintings, there is only one work, and *1965/1– ∞(detail: 868,149 – 893,746) c.*1968 is but a fragment of the set. At first, Opalka inscribed integers in white paint on a black background, but in 1968 he adopted a grey ground which he preferred for its neutrality. Humanity has always sought meaning from the chaos of existence through measurement of space and time. Opalka's project is both a testament to the futility of this action and an act of faith.

Douglas Huebler, who also involves himself in measurement, prefers to record his observations by more quotidian means than painting. His combination of photographs and words projects the seriousness of genuine research, even if the ambition might be an unrealisable ideal, such as photographing all of the people in the world, for example. He wrote:

> The world is full of objects, more or less interesting;
> I do not wish to add any more.
> I prefer, simply, to state the existence of things in terms of time and/or place.

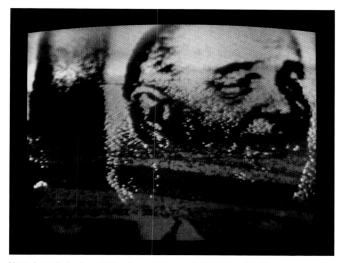

Nam June Paik from *Video tape study no. 3* 1967–69 videotape   **Bruce Nauman** from *Violin tuned D.E.A.D.* 1969 videotape

More specifically, the work concerns itself with things whose interrelationship is beyond direct perceptual experience.

Because the work is beyond direct perceptual experience, awareness of the work depends on a system of documentation.

This documentation takes the form of photography, maps, drawings and descriptive language.[13]

Location piece no. 2: New York City – Seattle, Washington 1969 is a work in which the idea of communication, verbal and visual, is investigated. Huebler directed a person in each city to take photographs in his or her area, which that person considered would match emotive words chosen by the artist. The photos, 'frightening', 'erotic', 'transcendent' and so on, were mixed together and a selection presented with maps of the area. Reading each image in the light of this knowledge completes the work.

As the need for presenting art in the form of physical objects declined, artists turned to their own bodies as material and subject for their art. Anyone could be an artist, every person their own ready-made. Bruce Nauman's *Self-portrait as a fountain* 1967 both recorded his own performance and showed the artist as the subject (and object) of his art.

Conceptual art, in making the idea of prime importance, focused attention on the artist as the generator of ideas. Performance art gave the artist a direct correspondence with the viewer; it was raw, honest and immediate. These advantages also worked against the artist by limiting the audience to those at the performance. Recording the action with photographs or videotape offered a way around this, and also historicised the event. More importantly, photography and videotaping transformed performance, mediating it to an already familiar information and entertainment format.

Television is undoubtedly the most persuasive of the new mass media. Nam June Paik attempted to distance himself from the existing 'look' of the medium, using magnets to distort the broadcast and generate abstract forms. But it was

more satisfying to subvert this, the most public channel of communication, by creating and showing private spectacle on television. In 1965 Paik was able to secure a Sony Portapak, the first personal video camera, and investigate the visual and formal qualities of this new technology.

In *Video tape study no. 3* 1967–69 Paik warps the image of US president Lyndon Baines Johnson into a diabolical presence. Altering the pace and synchronicity of the images and soundtrack, he transformed Johnson's speech into a revealing poem of comic desperation. Like Burn's *Xerox book*, Paik's video has been taped and retaped, celebrating the electronic intervention. *Beatles electronique* 1966–69 uses footage of the Beatles in concert, twisting and turning the images and sound into something entirely new. Electronic squiggles, spirals and lines swirl across the screen, syncopating to the beat of a tune created by the partnership of the Beatles, Paik and television.

Nauman capitalised on the documentary power of video to record his performance *Violin tuned D.E.A.D.* in 1969. Like Hesse, Nauman turned to his body as the ultimate referent in a world of unstable values. His image appears sideways on the screen, to make it more abstract. His back is to the audience, the viewer locked out of the artist's private struggle. There is no movement, other than the hand plucking a single note. The performance lasts for almost one hour — far longer than the attention span of the television audience. This is *real* time, not the compressed cinematic time of Hollywood. Nauman demonstrates a basic pattern of discord and endurance.

Permanent and cultural vibration

graffiti, Paris, May '68

The mind's eye

It seems ironic that some of the most severe and recondite high art movements of twentieth-century culture were co-opted and appropriated by the popular artists of acid rock. The clean optical geometry of Kinetic and Op artists such as Bridget Riley and Victor Vasarely was fertile ground for commercial artists in London and San Francisco who made posters and record covers for millions. Brilliant colour dissonances such as orange against blue or lime green versus purple, which were investigated in Op art, became part of the common visual language.

In *Gamelan* 1968, a watercolour study for her later painting, Bridget Riley uses the reverberation of pure colours, orange and green on white, mediated by lavender, to obtain a continuous ripple effect. The subtle play of stripes of varying widths forces the eye to wander up and down its length. Her title reflects the vast appeal of exotic cultures and Eastern religions at the time. The repetitive and dissonant percussion music of the gamelan orchestras of Bali and Java was appreciated for the first time in the West.

Other artists looked to the dazzling visual intricacies of Op art which emphasised perception, the 'eye' rather than the 'hand'. They wanted their works to look as though they could have been invented and manufactured by machines. The truly mechanical means of photography was seized on by Pop artists as one element to be used in their compositions. Others rejected photographic and figurative imagery in order to investigate the consequences of colour combinations.

In the later 1960s Riley returned to colour after the strict discipline of her black and white works. Earlier, colour had seemed a distraction. *Nineteen greys*, a set of screenprints made in 1968, shows the artist's growing interest in subtle effects of form and colour, and the interaction between them.

Vivienne Binns *Vag dens* 1967 synthetic polymer paint and enamel on composition board

The colours not only change within the varying oval forms, but between the works in the series. The deliberately unemotional, descriptive title does not attempt to give any extraneous meaning — neither does it convey the sensuous beauty of the prints.

Beginning in the mid-sixties, Alun Leach-Jones painted a series called *Noumenon*, colour variations on identical designs. The term was taken from philosophy, defined as 'an object of purely intellectual intuition'. Kant used noumenon as the opposite of a phenomenon, or thing perceived immediately through the senses. Leach-Jones was claiming much more than the visual impact of colours and forms, striking though these are. *Noumenon XXXII, Red square* 1968 becomes more complex the longer it is looked at. Red and pink squiggles, appearing to be cut in squares, form a circle on a ground of grey superimposed squares.

The influence of Josef Albers and his colour theories can be seen here, as well as Victor Vasarely's experiments with visual perception. Brown, purple and grey mediate the hot colours, so that the small figures seem to move, like the world of microbes revealed under the microscope. The artist's aim, as declared in his title, of going beyond the instant gratification of the senses, also fits with the contemporary desires to value intuition and to intensify experience.

Bruce Nauman's *Window or wall sign* 1967 is made of fluorescent tubes, familiar from decades of advertising. The sign moves between the public, exterior space of the street and the almost private, interior space of the gallery or museum. Nauman put it on display to the public by showing it in his studio window in San Francisco. Light and colour are encapsulated within glass, allowing the artist to write in the air, or on the wall, and giving a fuzzy, almost mystical glow to the sign. He chose the popular reverberating combination of hot candy pink and blue for his spiral message, which makes the viewer bend to decipher it. 'The true artist helps the world by revealing mystic truths', it declares, half ironically, in part longingly.

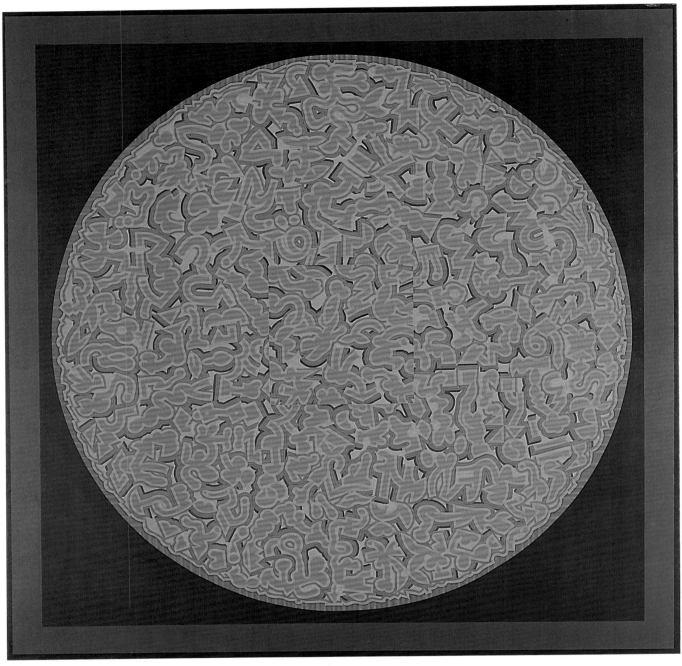

Alun Leach-Jones *Noumenon XXXII, Red square* 1968 synthetic polymer paint on canvas

Bruce Nauman *Window or wall sign* 1967 fluorescent tubes

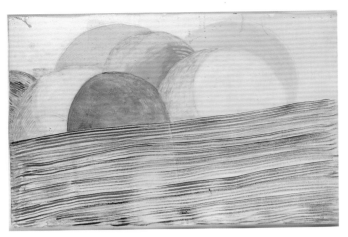 

Louise Bourgeois *Vallée de la rivière sans berge* [*Valley of the limitless river*] 1968 watercolour and chalk

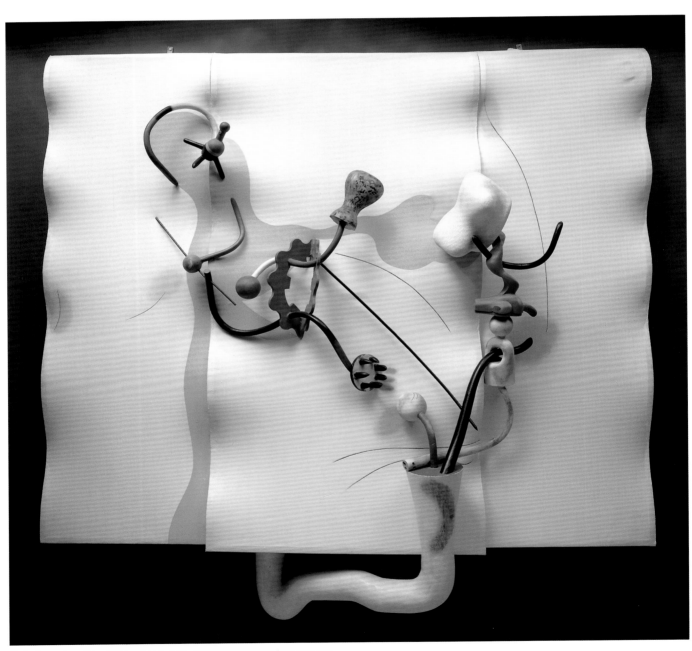

Colin Lanceley *Altar* 1967 painted wood, synthetic polymer paint on canvas

68

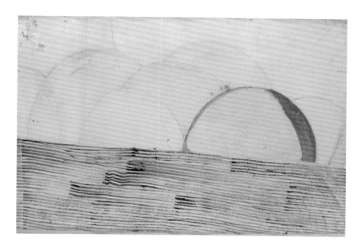

There was an ongoing debate about high art. What *use* is it? asked philistines, who were now joined by political and social rebels. 'Irrelevant' was the charge levelled at most art — a harsh reproof in the late sixties. The romantic banality of Nauman's slogan matches the vapid pseudo-mysticism of popular truisms such as the *Desiderata* or the verse of Rod McKuen. The point of the work, however, is that it must be appreciated for itself and for the ideas it generates, and Nauman reveals few truths. The viewer has to work for them, or just look at the beautiful effects of shimmering neon.

In 1968 the sculptor Louise Bourgeois drew *Vallée de la rivière sans berge* (literally 'Valley of the limitless river') with watercolour and chalk. Vivid primary colours are worked against whitened paper, like a mirage produced by extremes of heat and light. She connects the four drawings that make up the work by repeating the motifs of blue lines below semi-circular forms. These 'cumuls', as the artist calls them,

> are anthropomorphic and they are landscape also, since our body could be considered from a topographical point of view, as a land with mounds and valleys and caves and holes. It seems rather evident to me that our own body is a figuration that appears in Mother Earth.[14]

Bourgeois works in the idiom of abstract art, but her imagery is loaded with referents. She is a maverick, not tied to contemporary *isms*, following an independent path which is sometimes in tune with current fashions.

Colin Lanceley's first works engineered a clash between art and everyday artefacts. He then made constructions of wooden machine dies and moulds discarded by industry; these were often the negative shapes for casts, weirdly familiar though essentially unrecognisable. In *Altar* 1967 a number of these forms, vestiges of a tangible reality, are forced into a shotgun marriage with painted shapes on a canvas backdrop. The canvas is stretched into a wave-like profile which reconciles it with the three-dimensional elements. These objects, despite their machine sources (or perhaps because of them) take on the appearance of alien life forms, luxuriantly flowering in front of yellow and red

painted biomorphic shapes. From the bottom of the canvas, organic plumbing climbs up to climax in a flaring tuba mouth emitting a bouquet of notes. The triptych format may have prompted the title *Altar*, but if the painting honours any god it is Bacchus, such is its Monty Pythonesque zest and good-humoured exuberance.

Vivienne Binns created *Vag dens* in 1967. There is no comparable feminist or sexual work of art. Made a year before the first demonstration of the Women's Liberation Movement against a Miss America pageant at Jersey City in 1968, the painting argues the complexities of representation. Eyes and organs, little sperm, villi of nerve endings and mushrooms of papillae frame the vagina, surmounted by a heart of purple surrounded by rainbow ripples of joy. The crudely stroked paint reinforces the physicality of the subject.

The extraordinary impact of *Vag dens* comes from more than its bright, confrontational colouring. This is 'the personal is political' made flesh, or rather painted. A biological diagram of women's genitalia inscribed in funky, psychedelic hues, *Vag dens* scorns genteel metaphors from the past, such as Georgia O'Keeffe's flowers. 'Vagina dentata', the toothed vagina of Western patriarchal mythology, is here a celebration for women, although perhaps for male viewers it defines an arena of newly wary pleasure.

Bridget Riley *Study for **Gamelan*** 1968 gouache

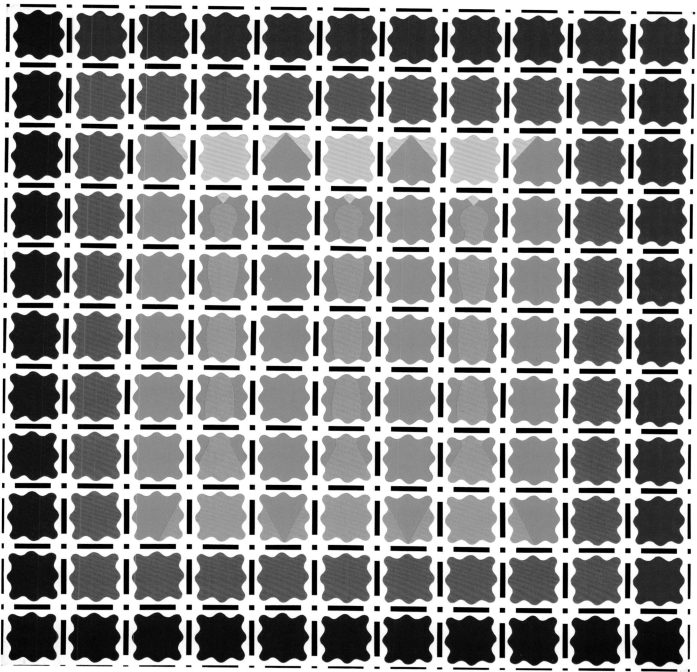

Robert Rooney *Kind-hearted kitchen-garden II* 1967 synthetic polymer paint on canvas

Art is dead.
Godard can't do
anything about it

Photography/Materiality

The end of the 1960s witnessed the adoption of photography as a major component of the language of high art. Although photography had superseded painting in the genre of portraiture in the nineteenth century, and as the means of recording historical events in the first half of the twentieth century, it was still resisted as a 'mechanical' technique until the iconoclasts of Pop art naturalised it in the sixties. Conservative critical and public voices yet saw 'the hand of the artist' as crucial. The craft skills of painters and sculptors who made unique objects were still prized highly.

For the rebels of 1968, it was the division between high and low art that had to be broken down. When artists such as Warhol used photographic means to 'manufacture' their works, it seemed to succeed in denying past cultural values. This art was mass currency, to be reproduced in multiple copies, available to anyone with a camera and a silkscreen. Everyone could be an artist, in control of their creativity, just as workers should control their labour.

Such claims for universality spread to include the sites for art. Showings in galleries and museums, or purchase by one private collector, meant exclusion and privileged ownership rather than universal good. What if the earth itself were to be the subject and the place for artworks at the same time? Earth Artists took art into the open air, and intervened in the surface of our planet. Offshoots included the use of found materials, rather than their facture by an artist. It was related to the wider movements of Conceptual art and *Arte povera*, especially in the argument that the idea was almost as important as, or even more meaningful than, its physical realisation.

Before wrapping the Kunsthalle in Bern, Switzerland in 1968, the artists Christo and Jeanne-Claude made plans to wrap up

one mile (1.6 km) of the Sydney coastline. Amidst local rejoicing and consternation, in 1969 Little Bay was enveloped in synthetic fabric, tied down with ropes and then released. It is one of the felicities of such art that it is reversible, to be returned to its former state. Drawings, plans, documentary photographs, films, books, and the memories of witnesses are the only things left to proclaim its existence.

Christo and Jeanne-Claude propose the wrapping of natural or artificial monuments of many cultures, and thereby to conceal, separate and somehow reveal them. According to the artists, their sculptures acknowledge the folds, pleats and veils of wood, bronze and stone art.[15] For some viewers, the packaging may recall the ordinary excitements of gift-wrapped birthday, Christmas or other festival presents, although on a huge scale. This is private experience in a public arena. The everyday pleasure of a parcel, with its half-guessed-at secrets, circumvents much of the normal disdain for arcane high art. While the contents are hidden, they are mysterious. After the work is dismantled, the subject/object is perceived anew, if only for a while.

The size and terrain of *Little Bay* allow enormous scope for the photographer, Harry Shunk, to record the project and its contemporary human impact. He also evokes the Romantic Alpine landscapes of Turner and, for Australians, von Guérard's 1863 depiction of his climbing of the continent's highest peak, Mount Kosciusko. Again, fine shadings of black and white tones distance the spectator. Viewing becomes contemplation. Banal physical practicalities — how much fabric? how many metres of rope? how many people to make it? are transcended by the sheer, unlikely beauty of the resulting landscape.

Richard Long also transgresses accepted norms of artistic representations of the land. *Ireland* 1967 witnesses the artist's mark upon the earth. Concentric circles are placed on

Larry Clark *Man on bed holding a gun* 1968 gelatin silver photograph

Christo and Jeanne-Claude (**Harry Shunk**, photographer) *Wrapped coast, one million square feet, Little Bay, Australia 1968–69* gelatin silver photograph 1969
Copyright Christo 1969

the ground, targeting previously unpublished territory. Because of Long's incursion, tension results due to the encounter between artificial and natural forms. Sometimes the artist walks from one place to another, photographing the territory he has covered. His absence from the resulting image is almost palpable.

Long attempts to make personal discoveries into artistic ones. 'Kilroy was here' is the ever-present graffito on city walls. Long was here, and by his presence captures the moment when he perceived the landscape. As an artist, he is our witness of an aesthetic, or of a normal experience not treasured enough in our world. By isolating it, he makes the moment a subject for thought.

Mapping or documenting an experience was one means of proclaiming the all-but-invisible function of the artist. Like Duchamp, Long argues that the presence of an artist is enough to make something into art. Selection is the paramount value here. The beautiful, almost sublime, photographs or sculptures resulting from much Conceptual and Minimal art are secondary considerations, say these artist-theoreticians.

There was an inherent conflict between the ephemeral nature of performance art and its documentation. Performance exists through time, while a photograph records a single moment, the time it takes the camera shutter to snap closed. Artists quickly realised that they could increase the audience by recording an action with film or photography. Just as importantly, the records of an action could be sold to offset the artwork's costs: the limitations of an 'unsaleable medium' could be overcome.

Bruce Nauman's *Self-portrait as a fountain* 1967 is not a random shot from a performance, but is consciously posed for the camera under coloured lights. Nauman capitalises on the ability of photography to freeze time, to make action static. A jet of water emerges from the artist's mouth, forever frozen as it arcs through space. This is a construction for the camera, a moment which can never be isolated by the eye.

Nauman's cheeky action is directed to us, the public, and to one of the masters of modern art, Marcel Duchamp. *Fountain*, the ready-made Duchamp exhibited in 1917, was a urinal turned on its side. By turning himself into an object, Nauman uses his body as the most basic ready-made,

Richard Long *Ireland* 1967 gelatin silver photograph

topping the master at his own game. Nauman's reference to the body as the font of art returns modernism to its sources.

Where Long and Nauman use photography as a documentary device, an integral part of their art but still a record of it, Arnulf Rainer intervenes in the medium itself. *Blaustern* [*Bluestar*] 1969 is a black and white self-portrait which the artist has attacked with blue crayon. Rainer's slashing strokes deface his image in an apparent attempt to obliterate identity. By mutilating the photograph, stabbing and smearing crayon over its smooth surface, he activates the work, liberating the image from its inert state. He seems to reassert his existence by repeatedly signing his name and the title.

Artists and musicians roamed the dark streets of contemporary urban culture, rubbing shoulders with its inhabitants — the junkies, prisoners, gangs and prostitutes. As with previous generations of bohemian artists, the underground was both their playground and their subject. To be straight was to be dead, in emotional terms. They loved flirting with danger.

Larry Clark's series *Tulsa* 1967–71 shows more than a process of documentation, the camera as witness. Beautiful gelatin silver photographs delineate a man toying with a gun on a bed in an anonymous room, tattooed arms shooting up heroin, or bondage sex with the artist as witness or participant. In *Man on bed holding a gun* 1968 he catches a

pensive mood, of someone considering possibilities, that seems more threatening than overt violence or self-destruction. This is the bad-boy image of James Dean, desanitised and presented as ordinary experience.

Clark also uses contemporary conventions such as serial images or repetitions recalling movie frames. In an untitled work of 1968 from *Tulsa*, two strips of contact prints are presented side by side. One sequence of images shows a grotesquely stitched arm, the other profiles a man's head in a car, with a desert view behind. Both subjects are anonymous and there is no explicit story. The artist forces a connection.

For Duane Michals, serial images imply narrative. The six photographs of *The human condition* 1969 read from left to right, like a book or comic strip. A man standing on a subway platform changes into a galaxy, in a gradual process of transmutation. The man's head fills with light as his consciousness expands and he becomes one with the universe. The artist's view of the human condition is visionary: we are born to die, but are offered the possibility of transcendence.

Danny Lyon's work is far from the cheerful and romanticised versions of middle-class life beloved of television and cinema. The images declare themselves in black and white, perhaps appearing to be starker, less emotional and more 'truthful' than colour photography. *Shakedown, Ramsey Prison Farm,*

Arnulf Rainer *Blaustern* [*Bluestar*] 1969 gelatin silver photograph, crayon

Danny Lyon *Shakedown, Ramsey Prison Farm, Texas* 1968 from *Conversations with the dead* 1967–68 gelatin silver photograph

20 July 1969: Edwin M. Aldrin walks on the moon
(Australian Picture Library/Bettmann)

Robert Rauschenberg *Banner* 1969 from *Stoned moon* 1969–70 lithograph

Texas 1967–68, while appearing to be a sober historical record, actually involves the viewer in the power struggle between the repressive state and the individual. The audience's sympathies are engaged, if not overtly by the photographic treatment, then by the subject: human beings stripped of their dignity.

Yousuf Karsh captured the passions and ideas of the late sixties in portraits which show cult musicians, politicians, astronauts and other heroes of technology in the same cool silvery light. The energy and discipline of *Ravi Shankar* on the sitar is made equivalent to the youthful premier of Canada, *Pierre Trudeau* in his leather coat. *Dr Christiaan Barnard*, who can transplant human hearts into new bodies, is a pioneer of technology like the spacemen who walk on the moon.

Robert Rauschenberg was invited by NASA to watch the launch of Apollo II as the spaceship set off for the moon in July 1969. He was one of very few artists to respond to the moon landing, producing *Stoned moon*, a large series of lithographs, in 1969–70. In *Banner* 1969, Rauschenberg indicates the launching site in Florida with his central image of oranges. The state seal of Florida evokes old conquests and discoveries, and carries the reassuring motto 'In God we trust'. NASA photographs of the new explorers and their rocket are eroded in their transfer to lithographic stone. In *Banner* they are pushed to the margins, the main theme of the series becoming a frame. Dissolving blue images of Apollo II are contrasted with the bright oranges, which remain in sharp focus, earthbound and material. The space program is an opportunity for the artist to let his imagination run loose, and the photographs are the visual trigger for free association.

Art doesn't exist.
Art is you

graffiti after Péret, Paris, May '68

The look: Art into fashion

In the 1950s and 1960s, style succeeded style and fad followed fad. The advertising industry sought novelties to fuel its insatiable appetite for increased consumption. One important source was science, another was art. The technologies of new inventions, the space race, computers and mass production delivered a clean world of plastic or inflatable furniture, lava lamps and white interiors, as well as fab gear. The pure geometry of Op art resonated in the severe haircuts of Vidal Sassoon, as well as striped tights and cutout dresses.

Pierre Cardin, like Courrèges and Paco Rabanne, looked to high art as well as popular culture for inspiration in the rarefied world of *haute couture*. He understood the stark principles of Utopian design to signify transformation of the female body. Twiggy (length without breadth) was the latest model phenomenon in swinging London, which threatened to replace Paris as the site of fashion.

Cardin's *Dress* of 1967 is a triangle of navy blue, relieved only by portholes in the skirt. White circles are revealed when the dress moves. Cardin's clothing is not suited to wealthy bourgeois matrons, as the female body is redefined in the starkest terms: thin, straight, without the curves of breasts or hips. Style and beauty depend on the rapid movements of youth culture.

Newly wearable materials, particularly plastics, rubber and metal, meant modernity in the mid-sixties. These are the materials that sculptors of Minimal art experimented with. Mary Quant tried red vinyl and plastic for shoes, while Paco Rabanne used grey and silver chainmail for his *Dance dress* c.1968. It reflects lights like the mirror balls in every discothèque. The dress is almost an abstraction — it is backless and skin-tight, with the shortest of miniskirts, a lowcut square neckline, a halterneck and cross-straps in the back.

Henry Talbot *Gilbey's Gin c*.1967–68 direct positive colour photograph

Henry Talbot is the stylish high-fashion photographer for a *Gilbey's Gin* advertisement c.1967–68. These are the beautiful people in Australia, not yet as trendy as London, inhabiting a white room in all-white clothes. Gin bottles and martini glasses stand on the clear table, a plastic cube. The only decoration is a green and purple circle, reminiscent of the round motifs of Kenneth Noland or the targets of Jasper Johns. The painter Janet Dawson designed her *Coffee table* 1968 with the same cool geometry, a two-toned circle of orange and beige laminex.

There was a new design for living. Curtains, wallpapers, carpets and rugs, chairs, tables and lamps shape the domestic environment, making a radical statement about taste and lifestyle. Interior design is now temporary, fashionable for a season, like hairstyles or handbags. Tennyson Textile Mills made bold furnishing fabrics inspired by Op art. *Circle* and *Circles* 1968 have large rings of bright red printed on a purple ground, or lime green on bright blue. Henry Talbot also accentuates the bold patterning of the era — stripes this time — in his *Maglia Knitwear* fashion shot of 1968. The jokey Wild West robbery is staged in a train, with movie-cliché Indians present.

As the decade ended, a softer style which fed on the anti-fashion look of the hippies came into being. The dropouts who rejected commerce, fashion and the consumer society fuelled the change to longer skirts, designs based on Indian and other 'ethnic' clothing, fabrics such as cotton, linen and undyed wool, and the 'natural' look in cosmetics. Their clothes signalled their 'outlaw' status, at odds with the conservative regimes in power. The trend setters and role models were rock musicians, pop artists and film stars. Style and youthful energy were more important than money and position.

Peter Fonda and Dennis Hopper ride their motorcycles like modern Vikings in the poster for the film *Easy rider* 1969, a two-and-a-half hour paean to personal freedom. Their long hair and fringed leather contrast with the constrictive formality

Janet Dawson *Coffee table* 1968 laminex on board

of their companion Jack Nicholson's middle-American jacket and tie. The seduction of middle-class values was nearly complete.

The Woodstock festival, held that year, was a celebration of the ascendancy of the alternative society. Many hallmarks of youth culture — electric music, mind-altering drugs, elaborate Victorian or simple hand-made garments, and nudity — were on show in a field in rural New York state. The Woodstock generation seemed to reject the high technology and commercialism of that most impressive monument to twentieth-century achievement, New York City. In a collision of two worlds, the pragmatic institutions of capitalism were beleaguered by the forces of idealism.

Capitalist society, however, was happy to buy its way out of the situation. 'The look' of youth culture was adopted by television, advertising, film and fashion, although not its underlying principles. At the end of the decade, radical chic appeared to displace radical ideas. The appropriation of rebellion as another marketing strategy allowed the cultural absorption, and finally the dissipation, of social and even political protest.

Paco Rabanne *Dance dress* c.1968 aluminium and silver

Yousuf Karsh *Ravi Shankar* *c.*1968 gelatin silver photograph

Fifteen hits of 1968
1 *Hey Jude* The Beatles
2 *Love Is Blue* Paul Mauriat
3 *Honey* Bobby Goldsboro
4 *People Got to Be Free* The Rascals
5 *Dock of the Bay* Otis Redding
6 *Love Child* Diana Ross & The Supremes
7 *This Guy's in Love with You* Herb Alpert
8 *The Good, the Bad and the Ugly* Hugo Montenegro
9 *Sunshine of Your Love* Cream
10 *Woman, Woman* The Union Gap
11 *Judy in Disguise* John Fred and His PlayboyBand
12 *Young Girl* Gary Puckett and The Union Gap
13 *Tighten Up* Archie Bell and the Drells
14 *Mrs Robinson* Simon & Garfunkel
15 *Little Green Apples* O.C. Smith

Number one Australian hit of 1968
Sadie the Cleaning Lady Johnny Farnham

R. Crumb *Cheap thrills* 1968 Big Brother and the Holding Company CBS

1967

If You're Going to San Francisco / All You Need Is Love/Penny Lane / Itchycoo Park / Strawberry Fields Forever / The Beat Goes On / Daydream Believer / The 59th St Bridge Song (Feelin' Groovy) / Alice's Restaurant / Light My Fire / Ode to Billy Joe / Ruby Tuesday / Up, Up and Away / For What It's Worth / Sock It to Me, Baby / Whiter Shade of Pale / The Who Sell Out / Disraeli Gears /Their Satanic Majesties Request / The Velvet Underground and Nico / Sergeant Pepper's Lonely Hearts Club Band

1968

Street Fighting Man / Hair / Good Morning Starshine / Aquarius / MacArthur Park / Wichita Linemen / The Windmills of Your Mind / Abraham, Martin & John / Jumpin' Jack Flash / Lady Madonna / White Album / Electric Ladyland / Astral Weeks / Two Virgins / Cheap Thrills / Beggars Banquet / Axis: Bold as Love / Wheels of Fire / Children of the Future / Ogden's Nut Gone Flake / The Archies / Trout Mask Replica / Anthem of the Sun

1969

Leaving on a Jet Plane / Lay Lady Lay / A Boy Named Sue / Get Back / Honky Tonk Women / Sugar Sugar / Happy Trails / Let it Bleed / Tommy / Nashville Skyline / Abbey Road / In the Court of the Crimson King

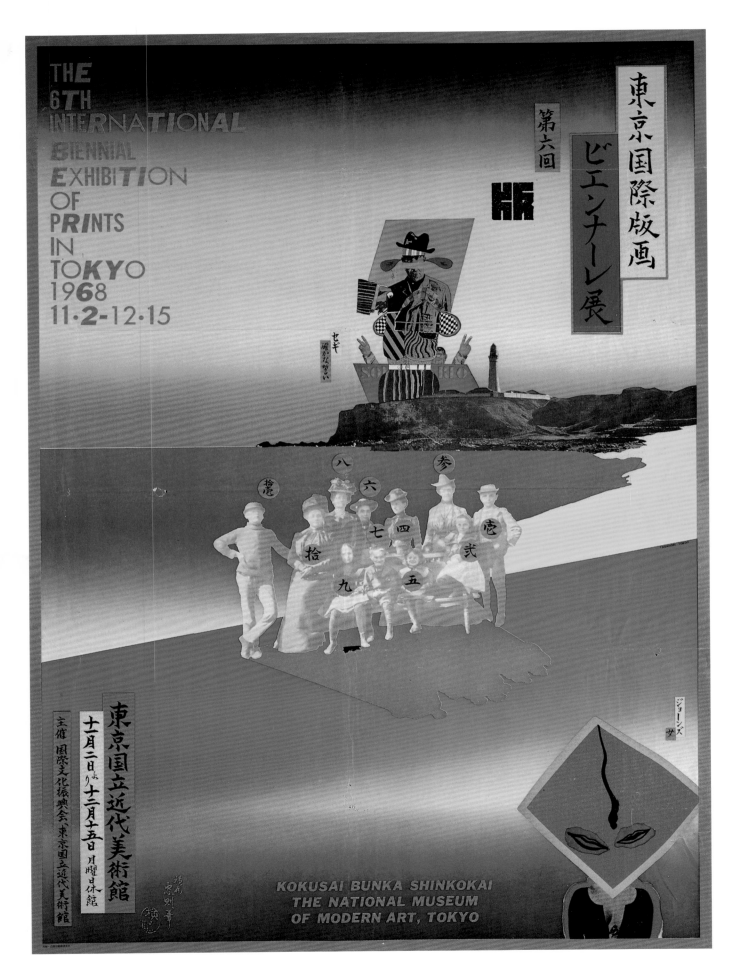

84

Imagination has seized power

graffiti, Paris, May '68

The legacy of 1968

The hopes and enthusiasms expressed in 1968 had a lasting impact. The year symbolises change, a moment when possibilities opened for many, a chance to transform old ways. Many of the ideas articulated and publicised in the late sixties had earlier sources, and these concerns continued into the next decades. By the mid-1970s, however, there were few signs of the large-scale dissent of 1968, apart from the growing strength of the pacifist and green movements, or leftover signs of hippiedom such as communes and long hair for men. The mass movements which had encompassed Western youth were over.

Besides a worldwide economic recession from the oil shock, it was the defeat of the South Vietnamese army in 1975, along with the Americans' inglorious flight from Vietnam, which showed that widespread revolt against the established order had finished. For many people, the horror of the Vietnam War was a major catalyst for revolt. When the war finally ended, the revolutionary impetus no longer existed.

In the 1970s, the idealistic fervour of the original cause was tainted by mindless acts of terrorist violence against civilians: aircraft hijackings, the Baader–Meinhof Red Army Faction in Germany, the Red Brigades in Italy, Shining Path guerrillas in Peru, and the kidnapping by Palestinians of Israeli athletes at the Munich Olympics in 1972.

The arts and society were transformed by the challenges of the sixties. It is possible, from the vantage point of the present, to compare the befores and afters, as if there were a discrete beginning and end. The cultural contests of the late sixties were part of an ongoing evolution, rather than a distinct revolution. The battles were hard fought and new concepts met considerable resistance before taking hold.

Yokoo Tadanori *6th International Biennial exhibition of prints in Tokyo* 1968 lithograph

In 1970 John Lennon was disillusioned by the small gains that had been made:

> The people who are in control and in power and the class system and the whole bullshit bourgeois scene is exactly the same except that there is a lot of middle-class kids with long hair walking around London in trendy clothes and Kenneth Tynan's made a fortune out of the word 'fuck'. But apart from that, nothing happened except that we all dressed up. The same bastards are in control, the same people are running everything, it's exactly the same. They hyped the kids and the generation ... there has been a change and we are a bit freer and all that, but it's the same game, nothing's really changed.[16]

For many artists, the radical artistic experiments of the late sixties and early seventies had led to a new academy. The art market and museums showed that they could appropriate this one too. The audience for this kind of contemporary art was smaller than ever, sometimes seeming to consist only of the participants. Much of the art being made seemed to exclude ordinary people.

Parallel with rarefied avant-garde art, new audiences were being sought by artists who appreciated the strategies of the sixties. Instead of the endless variations of modernism, art for art's sake, they attempted to link the myriad means discovered in the previous decade with social ends. Mary Kelly's *Post-partum document* 1973–78 relies on the notational approach of Conceptual art, but her subject is the publication of female experience.

Performance, installation and video art become dominant art forms in the 1970s. In 1973, branding the word 'artist' on his thigh, Mike Parr made his own body into the field for his art. Once any experience is as valid as the next, then the criteria of 'quality' and 'good taste' become irrelevant. Categories such as painting or sculpture no longer apply.

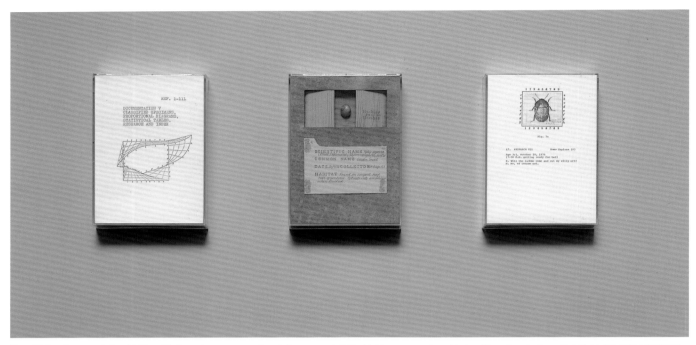

Mary Kelly *Documentation V: Classified specimens, proportional diagrams, statistical tables, research and index (Experimentum mentus V: on the order of things)* 1977 from *Post-partum document* 1974–79 mixed media

Artists had thumbed their noses at the commercial galleries, museums and the public, in creating art forms that denied an object to be bought or sold. By the mid-seventies such defiance seemed rhetorical, as 'unsaleable' works exchanged hands in the art market. 'Not only do works of art end up as commodities,' wrote Ian Burn in 1975, 'but there is also an overwhelming sense in which works of art *start off* as commodities.'[17] Such disenchantment was rare (the art establishment and the avant-garde had kissed and made up) and most people got on with business. Capitalism had resisted the challenge to its hegemony in the arts as elsewhere in society.

As well as making work for sale, artists exploited the breakthroughs and innovations that had been made. The intense experimentation that characterised the sixties was consolidated in the seventies. New materials as well as new approaches to art-making gave artists rich veins to mine. Performance, video, photography, Photorealism, pattern painting, feminist art, Hispanic art, and art by black artists were produced alongside Minimal and Conceptual art. With no single model dominant, the very idea of an avant-garde was under severe threat.

Central to the notion of the 'avant-garde' is a distinction between 'high' and 'low' art. At the beginning of the sixties this was understood as 'art' and 'non-art' but by the end of the decade the more inclusive terms were used. The year 1968 marked the high tide of formalism and the return of content to art — communication of information rather than construction of style. Feminist art, for example, subordinated style to political aims. Incorporating elements of 'low' art (illustration, advertisements, comics and so on) into the mainstream offered an enlarged vocabulary and greater opportunities to engage the public.

By the end of the sixties it was acknowledged that art is produced in a context of social, political and intellectual ideas and beliefs. Forcing museums and galleries to accommodate women, blacks and others in exhibitions demonstrated just how art history could be rewritten to include rather than exclude. Today, art is understood to be fluid and complex, connected with other stories. Art's history is seen as relative and partial, which is a particular legacy of the sixties' social program for art.

1968 is a fulcrum, the balancing point between 'modern' and 'post-modern'. The optimistic experiment of modernist art was modified by a recognition of the impossibility of the venture. Attempts by artists in the twentieth century to break down the restrictions of media and materials had succeeded to their logical point, where the boundaries of art itself were seen to dissolve. Art's traditional cultural purposes, of communication and the circulation of visual ideas, were superseded by mass media, especially television and film.

Thereafter, contemporary artists were left in the position of commenting on past art, or ironising about their own creative production. Liberated from their burdens as bearers of culture, artists felt free to reject the common ground of modernism. The end of certainty allowed new voices to speak, sparked an increased perception of other cultures, and encouraged exchanges of information.

McLuhan wrote in 1967:
> We now live in a *global* village ... At the high speeds of electric communication, purely visual means of apprehending the world are no longer possible; they are just too slow to be relevant or effective.[18]

Larry Clark *Multiple images* 1968 gelatin silver photograph

In the sixties, contemporary art obeyed this law. The role of the arts seemed to be supplanted by technology, although McLuhan did not predict the extraordinary advances in computing. Traditional 'visual means of apprehending the world' — looking at static, silent images or words — can be incorporated into universal electronic media. Artists, like others, may take advantage of the opportunities that arise with the rapid communication of information, ideas and images.

The great legacy of the sixties is the pluralism which animated social movements into the following decades — feminism, pacifism, anti-nuclear movements, community action against pollution and bureaucracy — personal and local concerns which involved many people in political and cultural action. In the 1960s, like everyone else, artists tested the limits of authority. No longer is it possible to believe that the government knows best, that science is infallible, that wisdom resides with the old order, or that alternative paths are impossible. The liberation that follows is the main testament of 1968.

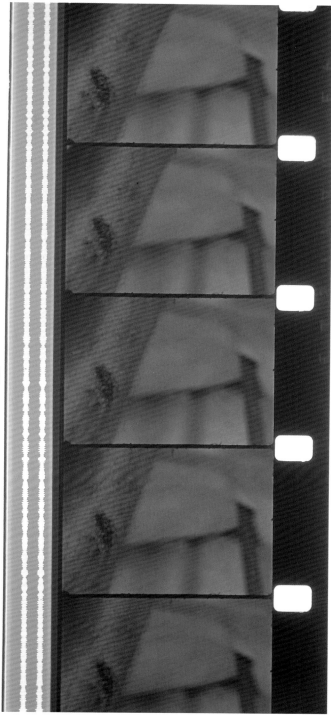

Mike Parr from *Rules and displacement activities I* 1973–74 film

Notes

The graffiti from Paris, May 1968, is recorded in Marc Rohan, *Paris '68*, London: Impact, 1988.

1.   Stephen Stills, *For What It's Worth*, 1967

2.   James Rado and Gerome Ragni, *Hair*, 1968

3.   Wes Wilson, quoted in Paul D. Grushkin, *The Art of Rock: Posters from Presley to Punk*, New York: Abbeville Press, 1987, p.73

4.   Bill Graham, quoted in Grushkin, p.73

5.   Leo Steinberg, reprinted in *Other Criteria: Confrontations with Twentieth Century Art*, London, Oxford, New York: Oxford University Press, 1972, p.84

6.   Herbert Marcuse, *An Essay on Liberation*, Boston: Beacon Press, 1969, p.8

7.   Quoted in Chris Wallace-Crabbe, 'Two decades of American painting', *Art in Australia*, September 1967, p.422

8.   Clement Greenberg, 'Recentness of sculpture', *Art International*, April 1967, pp.19–21

9.   Michael Fried, 'Art and objecthood', *Artforum*, June 1967, p.125

10. Interview with Richard Serra by Bernard Lamarche-Vidal, New York, 1980, in *Richard Serra: Interviews, etc., 1970–1980*, Yonkers NY: Hudson River Museum, 1980, p.142

11. Robert Morris, 'Anti form', *Artforum*, April 1968, p.35

12. The artist, quoted in Alicia Legg (ed.), *Sol LeWitt*, New York: Museum of Modern Art, 1978, p.166

13. Douglas Huebler, *January 5–31, 1969*, New York: Seth Siegelaub, 1969, no page numbering

14. Interview with the artist, 14 October 1981, quoted in Deborah Wye, *Louise Bourgeois*, New York: Museum of Modern Art, 1982, p.25

15. Conversation with Jeanne-Claude, 18 May 1995

16. From J. Wenner, *Lennon Remembers: The Rolling Stone Interviews*, Harmondsworth: Penguin, 1972, quoted in Bart Moore-Gilbert and John Seed, *Cultural Revolution? The Challenge of the Arts in the 1960s*, London and New York: Routledge, 1992, pp.3–4

17. Ian Burn, 'The art market: affluence and degradation', *Artforum*, April 1975, p.35

18. Marshall McLuhan and Quentin Fiore, *The Medium is the Massage*, Harmondsworth: Penguin, 1967, p.63

Copyright acknowledgements

The publisher wishes to thank all copyright owners for permission to publish. Specific by-lines are as below:

© Carl Andre/DACS, London/VAGA, New York 1995

Diane Arbus © Estate of Diane Arbus 1971

© Louise Bourgeois/DACS, London/VAGA, New York 1995

Ian Burn © Estate of Ian Burn

© Patrick Caulfield 1995 All rights reserved DACS

Janet Dawson works reproduced by permission of the artist

© Richard Hamilton 1995 All rights reserved DACS

© Jasper Johns/DACS, London/VAGA, New York 1995

© Roy Lichtenstein/DACS 1995

© Danny Lyon/Magnum Photos 1995

© Robert Rauschenberg/DACS, London/VAGA, New York 1995

© Arnold Skolnick/DACS, London/VAGA, New York 1995

© Joe Tilson 1995 All rights reserved DACS

© Wesley Stacey 1995

© 1996 Dan Flavin/Artists Rights Society (ARS), New York

© 1996 Douglas Heubler/Artists Rights Society (ARS), New York

© 1996 Sol LeWitt/Artists Rights Society (ARS), New York

© 1996 Robert Morris/Artists Rights Society (ARS), New York

© 1996 Bruce Nauman/Artists Rights Society (ARS), New York

© 1996 Richard Serra/Artists Rights Society (ARS), New York

© 1996 Andy Warhol Foundation for the Visual Arts/ARS, New York

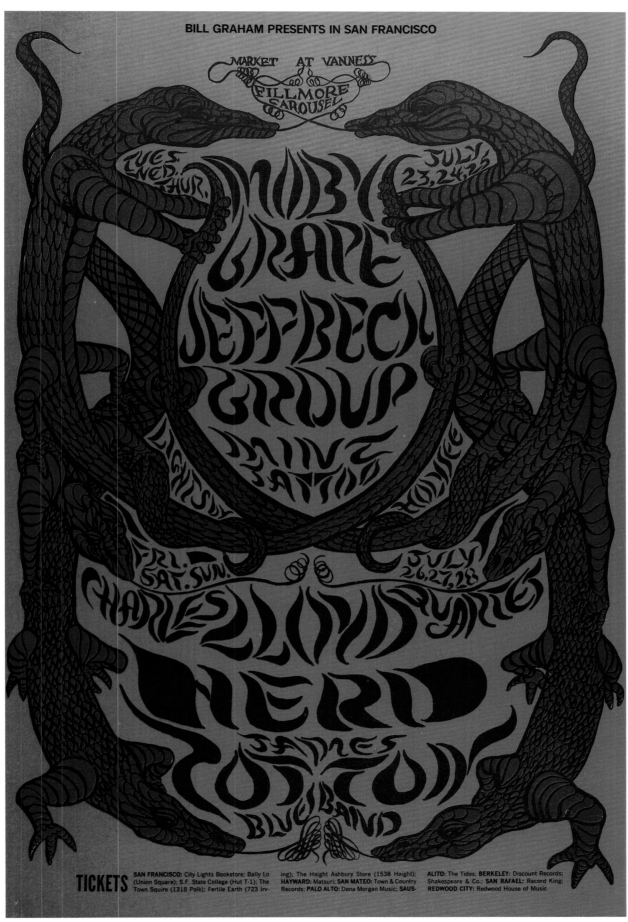

Lee Conklin *Moby Grape/Jeff Beck Group/Mint Tattoo* 1968 lithograph

Checklist

All works in the exhibition are in the collection of the National Gallery of Australia, Canberra. Measurements are in centimetres, height x width, and for three-dimensional works, height x width x depth. Editions are given where known.

Joyce ALLEN
Australia 1916–1992
Up and down. 1968
linocut
71.8 x 43.0 cm
1 of 3 artist's proofs (edition 15)
Purchased 1987   1987.390

Carl ANDRE
United States born 1935
Untitled.
from *Carl Andre, Robert Barry, Douglas Huebler, Joseph Kosuth, Sol LeWitt, Robert Morris, Lawrence Weiner*
New York: Seth Siegelaub 1968
photocopy
28.0 x 21.4 cm (page)
Purchased 1981   1981.1718

Diane ARBUS
United States 1923–1971
Boy with a straw hat waiting to march in a pro-war parade, N.Y.C., 1967. 1967
gelatin silver photograph
39.6 x 38.4 cm
Purchased 1980   1980.3559

Patriotic young man with a flag, N.Y.C. 1967
gelatin silver photograph
39.6 x 38.0 cm
Purchased 1980   1980.3557

Black family, Beaufort County, S.C., 1968
1968
gelatin silver photograph
26.4 x 25.0 cm
Purchased 1981   1981.1600

(Old black woman with gnarled hand). 1968
gelatin silver photograph
27.1 x 26.4 cm
Purchased 1981   1981.1586

ART WORKERS COALITION
United States
Ronald HAEBERLE, photographer
United States working 1960s
Poster: *Q. And babies? A. And babies.*
1969
colour photolithograph
63.5 x 93.5 cm
edition 50,000
Proposed purchase 1995

Jo BAER
United States born 1929
Untitled (vertical flanking diptych — red).
1966–74
oil on two canvases
244.0 x 172.7 cm each; 244.0 x 376.0 cm overall
Purchased 1973   1973.819.A–B

Vivienne BINNS
Australia born 1940
Vag dens. 1967
synthetic polymer paint and enamel on composition board
122.0 x 91.5 cm
Purchased 1978   1978.1302

Louise BOURGEOIS
France born 1911, to United States 1939
Vallée de la rivière sans berge. [*Valley of the limitless river.*] 1968
watercolour and chalk on four sheets
69.2 x 436.9 cm overall
Purchased 1988   1989.351.A–D

Ian BURN
Australia 1939–1993
also worked in the United States
Undeclared glass. 1967
letterpress, glass
57.0 x 73.8 cm (print); 150.0 x 50.0 x 0.6 cm (glass); 150.0 x 166.0 x 10.0 cm overall (variable)
edition 12/13
Purchased 1978   1978.846

Xerox book
New York: The artist 1968
photocopy
21.2 x 27.6 cm (page)
Purchased 1978   1978.847

'Dialogue'
in *Untitled*
New York: Art Press 1969
photocopy
28.0 x 21.4 cm (page)
Gift of Bruce Pollard 1979   1979.2304

Pierre CARDIN
Italy born 1922, to France 1924
Apron dress. c.1967
leather, metal
length 79.4 cm
Purchased 1993   1993.98

Dress. c.1967
wool
length 84.2 cm
Purchased 1994   1994.1407

Patrick CAULFIELD
Great Britain born 1936
Bathroom mirror. 1968
colour screenprint
71.1 x 93.6 cm
edition 30/75
Purchased 1972   1972.326

Café sign. 1968
colour screenprint
71.2 x 93.4 cm
edition 62/75
Purchased 1978   1978.1005

Loudspeaker. 1968
colour screenprint
71.0 x 93.0 cm
edition 19/75
Purchased 1978   1978.1004

Rich CHARTER
working 1960s
Poster for *Rolling Stones.* 1967
colour screenprint
58.6 x 44.4 cm
Purchased 1978   1978.255.45

Gunter CHRISTMANN
born Germany 1936, to Australia 1959
Big black. 1969
synthetic polymer paint on canvas
168.0 x 272.0 cm
Purchased 1977   1977.170

CHRISTO
Bulgaria born 1935, working in New York since 1964
Packed coast (Project for Australia near Sydney). 1969
collage of fabric, plastic, twine, photographs, pencil, charcoal, crayon 71.0 x 55.8 cm
Purchased 1972   1972.42

CHRISTO and JEANNE-CLAUDE
Bulgaria born 1935, working in New York since 1964
born 1935, working in New York since 1964
Harry SHUNK, photographer
Italy born 1942
Wrapped coast, one million square feet, Little Bay Australia, 1968–69. 1969
gelatin silver photograph
101.5 x 127.0 cm
Gift of John Kaldor 1982   1983.9

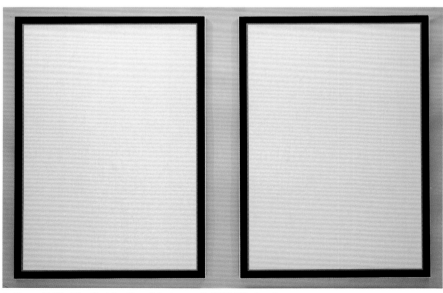

Jo Baer *Untitled (vertical flanking diptych — red)* 1966–74 oil on two canvases

Larry CLARK
United States born 1943
from *Tulsa* 1963–71
    (*Man on bed holding a gun*). 1968
    31.3 x 20.4 cm 1980.207
    (*Multiple images*). 1968
    35.3 x 27.8 cm 1980.3291.19
gelatin silver photographs
Purchased 1980

Lee CONKLIN
United States born 1941 working 1960s
Poster for *Moby Grape/Jeff Beck Group/Mint
Tattoo*. 1968
colour lithograph
53.8 x 35.8 cm
Purchased 1978   1978.255.137

Poster for *Santana/Youngbloods/All Men Joy*.
1969
colour lithograph
35.8 x 53.8 cm
Purchased 1978   1978.255.341

Lee CONKLIN
Herb GREENE, photographer
United States working 1960s
Poster for *Grateful Dead/Pentangle/Sir
Douglas Quintet*. 1969
colour lithograph
53.4 x 35.6 cm
Purchased 1978   1978.255.276

R. CRUMB
United States born 1943
Zap Comix No.0 October 1967
colour lithograph
24.6 x 17.2 cm (page)
Gift of Lanier Graham 1987   1987.2214

Zap Comix No.1 November 1967
colour lithograph
25.0 x 17.3 cm (page)
Gift of Lanier Graham 1987   1987.2215

Zap Comix No.2 1968
colour lithograph
24.8 x 17.3 cm (page)
Gift of Lanier Graham 1987   1987.2216

Janet DAWSON
Australia born 1935
Wall II. 1968–69
synthetic polymer paint on canvas
183.0 x 183.0 cm
Purchased 1969   1969.88

Coffee table. 1968
laminex on board
43.0 x 122.0 cm (diameter)
Purchased 1983   1983.3097

Dan FLAVIN
United States born 1933
monument to V. Tatlin. 1966–69
fluorescent tubes
274.5 x 71.0 x 11.3 cm
edition 3/5
Purchased 1977   1978.386

Robert FRIED
United States died 1975
Poster for *The High Mass is coming in
November*. 1967
colour lithograph
69.0 x 54.0 cm
Purchased 1978   1978.255.50

Poster for *Steppenwolf/Charley Musselwhite/
The 4th Way/Indian Head Band*. 1968
colour lithograph
54.2 x 35.5 cm
Purchased 1978   1978.255.489

Kevin GILBERT
Australia 1933–1993
The nomad. 1967, printed 1990
linocut
35.0 x 35.0 cm
edition 17/50
Gordon Darling Fund 1990   1990.747

*Christmas Eve in the land of the
dispossessed*. 1969, printed 1990
linocut
45.0 x 63.1 cm
edition 7/50
Gordon Darling Fund 1990   1990.756

THE GRAPHICS COMMUNITY
working 1960s
GLEESON-GURNEY, photographer
Poster for *The Beatles*. 1967
colour screenprint
58.5 x 44.6 cm
Purchased 1978   1978.255.46

Rick GRIFFIN
United States 1944–1991
Poster for *Joint show*. 1967
colour lithograph
70.7 x 55.9 cm
edition 1,200
Purchased 1978   1978.255.53

Poster for *Bulls Eye/Albert King/Creedence
Clearwater Revival*. 1968
colour lithograph
35.6 x 56.0 cm
Purchased 1978   1978.255.159

Poster for *The Who/Poco/The Bonzo Dog
Band*. 1969
colour lithograph
57.4 x 44.0 cm
Purchased 1978   1978.255.256

Richard HAMILTON
Great Britain born 1922
Toaster. 1967
colour lithograph, screenprint, metallised
polymer film
89.0 x 63.6 cm
edition 61/75
Purchased 1982   1982.2234

Eva HESSE
Germany 1936 – United States 1970
Contingent. 1969
cheesecloth, latex, fibreglass
368.5 x 630.0 x 109.0 cm overall
Purchased 1973   1974.395

Dale HICKEY
Australia born 1937
Atlantis wall. 1969
synthetic polymer paint on two canvases
213.7 x 427.4 cm overall
Purchased 1979   1979.2546

Unknown artist (**Bill Bractis**, photographer) *Moby Grape/Its a Beautiful Day/The Other Half/Tim Hardin/Jerry Abrams* 1969 lithograph

Douglas HUEBLER
United States born 1924
*Location piece no. 2: New York City–Seattle,
Washington* July 1969
New York: Multiples Inc. 1970
photolithographs
17.8 x 17.8 cm
Purchased 1982   1982.2137.17

Robert HUNTER
Australia born 1947
Untitled. 1968
synthetic polymer paint on canvas
215.0 x 215.0 cm
Purchased 1969   1969.146

Robert JACKS
Australia born 1943
also worked in the United States
1–12
New York: The artist 1969
(book) lineblock
9.3 x 5.2 cm
Purchased 1977   1977.1030–1977.1031

Paper. 1969
cut paper
182.5 x 122.3 x 18.0 cm (variable)
Purchased 1979   1979.2565

Rubber. 1969
cut rubber
61.4 x 119.5 x 0.4 cm
Purchased 1979   1979.2566

Jasper JOHNS
United States born 1930
from *Lead reliefs* 1969
    Bread
    lead, paper and oil paint
    58.9 cm x 43.6 cm
    The critic smiles
    lead, gold, tin
    58.8 x 43.5 cm
    High school days
    58.5 x 43.5 cm
    lead, mirror
    Light bulb
    lead
    99.3 cm x 43.3 cm
right to print proofs (edition 60)
Purchased 1973   1973.1057–1058,
                    1978.1060–1061

Michael JOHNSON
Australia born 1938
Frontal red. 1969
synthetic polymer paint on shaped canvas
213.2 x 198.6 cm
Purchased 1970   1970.112

Allen JONES
Great Britain born 1937
from *Life class.* 1968
lithographs, photolithographs
68.6 x 56.4 cm
edition 51/75
Purchased 1984   1984.187.1–8

Yousuf KARSH
Canada born 1908
Pierre Elliott Trudeau. 1968
gelatin silver photograph
99.0 x 73.6 cm
Purchased 1973   1974.396.18

Colonel John Glenn. c.1968
gelatin silver photograph
99.0 x 73.6 cm
Purchased 1973   1974.396.50

Dr Christiaan Barnard. c.1968
gelatin silver photograph
99.0 x 73.6 cm
Purchased 1973   1974.396.128

Ravi Shankar. c.1968
gelatin silver photograph
99.0 x 73.6 cm
Purchased 1973   1974.396.51

*The Apollo 11 crew: Astronauts Neil
Armstrong, Edwin Aldrin, Michael Collins.*
1969
gelatin silver photograph
27.4 x 35.0 cm
Purchased 1973   1974.396.81

Colin LANCELEY
New Zealand born 1938, to Australia 1940
also worked in Great Britain
Altar. 1967
painted wood, synthetic polymer paint on
canvas
183.0 x 249.0 x 33.0 cm
Purchased 1976   1976.552

Bluebeard's castle. 1968
colour screenprint
101.5 x 68.0 cm
artist's proof 23/30
Purchased 1972   1972.600

Richard LARTER
Great Britain born 1929, to Australia 1962
Big time easy mix. 1969
synthetic polymer paint on composition board
122.2 x 183.3 cm
Gift of the Philip Morris Arts Grant 1982
1983.1549

Alun LEACH-JONES
Great Britain born 1937, to Australia 1960
Noumenon XXXII, Red square. 1968
synthetic polymer paint on canvas
168.5 x 168.5 cm
Purchased 1969   1969.91

Nigel LENDON
Australia born 1944
Untitled floor structure 1969—1. 1969
painted wood
29.4 x 175.0 x 175.0 cm
Purchased 1969   1969.101

Sol LeWITT
United States born 1928
Cubic modular piece no. 3. 1968
synthetic polymer paint on steel
232.2 x 277.2 x 50.0 cm
Purchased 1977   1978.383

'Sentences on Conceptual Art'
in *Art — Language* vol. 1, no. 1
Leamington Spa: Art and Language
Press 1969
photolithograph
21.0 x 14.2 cm (page)
Purchased 1981   1981.891

Roy LICHTENSTEIN
United States born 1923
Brushstrokes. 1967
colour screenprint
55.6 x 76.3 cm
edition 189/300
Purchased 1983   1983.1472

Richard LONG
Great Britain born 1945
Ireland. 1967
gelatin silver photograph
33.2 x 50.6 cm
Purchased 1982   1982.1368

Danny LYON
United States born 1924
from *Conversations with the dead* 1967–68
    *Shakedown, Ramsey Prison Farm,
    Texas.* 1968
    16.3 x 24.0 cm
    *Six-wing cell block, Ramsey Prison
    Farm, Texas.* 1968
    16.1 x 24.0 cm
gelatin silver photographs
Purchased 1994   1994.1361–2

Duane MICHALS
United States born 1932
The human condition. 1969
gelatin silver photographs
12.6 x 17.6 cm each; 12.6 x 105.6 cm overall
edition 12/15
Purchased 1983   1983.107.A–F

Robert MORRIS
United States born 1931
Untitled. 1969
felt
284.0 x 363.2 x 111.8 cm
Purchased 1975   1975.152

Victor MOSCOSO
Spain born 1936   works in the United States
Poster for *Blue Cheer/Lee Michaels/North
America.* 1967
colour lithograph
50.8 x 35.6 cm
Purchased 1978   1978.255.506

Mary Quant *Shoes* c.1967 vinyl, plastic, metal fittings

Victor MOSCOSO
Paul KAGAN, photographer
Poster for *Youngbloods/The Other Half/Mad River*. 1967
colour lithograph
50.8 x 35.6 cm
Purchased 1978   1978.255.509

Stanley MOUSE
United States working 1960s
Poster for *Love/Congress of Wonders/Sons of Champlin*. 1968
colour lithograph
50.7 x 31.1 cm
Purchased 1978   1978.255.495

Stanley MOUSE
Alton KELLEY
United States working 1960s
Poster for *Miller Blues Band/Mother Earth*. 1967
colour lithograph
50.8 x 35.6 cm
Purchased 1978   1978.255.512

Bruce NAUMAN
United States born 1941
Self-portrait as a fountain. 1967
from *Eleven color photographs* 1966/67–1970, printed 1980
type C photograph
50.0 x 60.4 cm
edition 2/8
Purchased 1978   1978.982.7

Window or wall sign. 1967
fluorescent tubes
149.9 x 134.7 cm
edition of 3
Purchased 1978   1978.976

Violin tuned D.E.A.D. 1969
videotape, sound, 55 minutes
Purchased 1983   1983.2944

Claes OLDENBURG
Sweden born 1929, to the United States 1936
Miniature soft drum set. 1969
printed canvas, rope, wood and wooden box
31.0 x 51.0 x 35.8 cm (variable)
edition 23/200
Purchased 1979   1980.746

Profile airflow. 1969
polyurethane relief over colour lithograph
82.8 x 164.1 x 6.0 cm
right to print proof (edition 75)
Purchased 1973   1973.908.2

Yoko ONO
Japan born 1933, to the United States 1953
Bottoms wallpaper. c.1968
photolithographs
56.6 x 43.2 cm each
Gift of Alan R. Dodge and Gilbert Silverman 1993   1993.527.1–25

Roman OPALKA
France born 1931
also worked in Poland
1965/1–∞ (detail 868,149 – 893,746). c.1968
synthetic polymer paint on canvas
196.8 x 135.3 cm
Purchased 1978   1978.973

Nam June PAIK
Korea born 1932, to the United States 1964
also worked in Japan and Germany
Beatles electronique. 1966–69
videotape, sound, 3 minutes
Purchased 1995   1995.132.1

Video tape study no. 3. 1967–69
videotape, sound, 4 minutes
Purchased 1995   1995.132.2

Paul PARTOS
Czechoslovakia born 1943, to Australia 1949
Yellow screen with yellow. 1968
painted nylon and wood
274.0 x 107.5 x 31.0 cm
Purchased 1972   1972.315

Black screen. 1968–69
painted nylon and wood
274.0 x 107.5 x 31.0 cm
Purchased 1973   1973.28

Mary QUANT
Great Britain born 1934
Shoes. c.1967
vinyl, plastic, metal fittings
10.2 x 25.0 x 8.4 cm
Purchased 1992   1992.1125

Paco RABANNE
Spain born 1934, to France 1939
Dance dress. c.1968
aluminium and silver
length 57.8 cm excluding straps
Purchased 1984   1984.1147

Arnulf RAINER
Austria born 1929
Blaustern. [*Bluestar*.] 1969
gelatin silver photograph, crayon
59.6 x 50.0 cm
Purchased 1982   1982.2264

Unknown artist *Haight* c.1967 screenprint

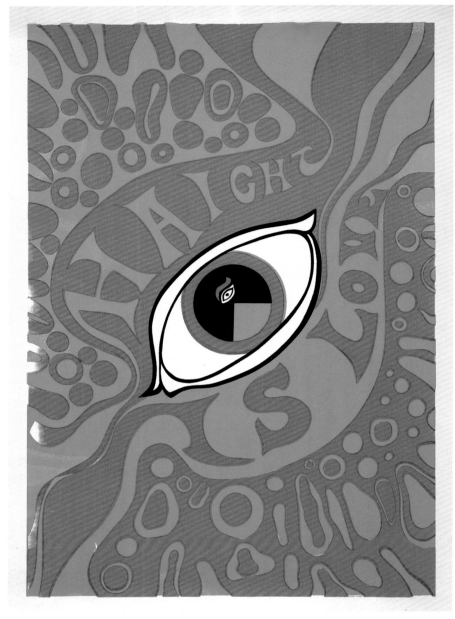

Unknown artist after **John Cleveland** *Haight is love* c.1967 screenprint

Mel RAMSDEN
Great Britain born 1944, to the United States 1967
Guarantee painting. 1967–68
oil on canvas with a gelatin silver photograph
25.2 x 25.2 cm (painting); 63.0 x 63.0 cm (photograph); 63.0 x 138.0 cm overall
Purchased 1979   1979.2544

Robert RAUSCHENBERG
United States born 1925
Booster.
from *Booster and seven studies.* 1967
colour lithograph, screenprint
183.0 x 89.0 cm
right to print proof (edition 38)
Purchased 1973   1973.927

Banner. 1969
from *Stoned moon* 1969–70
colour lithograph
137.2 x 91.4 cm
right to print proof (edition 40)
Purchased 1973   1973.1163

Bridget RILEY
Great Britain born 1931
from *Nineteen greys.* 1968
   B.
   76.0 x 75.0 cm
   D.
   75.8 x 75.9 cm
colour screenprints on card
edition 32/75
Purchased 1972   1972.327–328

Study for **Gamelan**. 1968
gouache
67.6 x 102.2 cm
Purchased 1979   1980.106

Robert ROONEY
Australia born 1937
Kind-hearted kitchen-garden II. 1967
synthetic polymer paint on canvas
167.9 x 168.1 cm
Purchased 1979   1979.2547

Alfredo ROSTGAARD
Cuba working 1960s
Poster for *Hasta la victoria siempre.* [*Until the final victory.*] 1968
colour screenprint
76.1 x 50.6 cm
Gift of Chips Mackinolty 1989 1989.1743

Richard SERRA
United States born 1939
Prop. 1968
lead
152.4 x 152.4 x 243.5 cm
Purchased 1973   1975.670

Martin SHARP
Australia born 1942
Jimi Hendrix. 1968
enamel on synthetic polymer film
101.0 x 115.0 cm
Gift of Jim Sharman 1984   1984.1543

Mister tambourine man. 1968
colour screenprint on foil paper
76.1 x 50.8 cm
Purchased 1972   1972.12.4

Poster: *Sunshine superman.* 1968
colour screenprint on foil paper
74.1 x 49.6 cm
Purchased 1972   1972.12.2

Vincent. 1968
colour photolithograph
73.4 x 49.2 cm
Purchased 1972   1972.12.3

Arnold SKOLNICK
United States working 1960s
3 days of peace & music. 1969
poster for the Woodstock Music and Art Fair, New York State
colour screenprint
66.8 x 51.2 cm
Purchased 1978   1978.255.344

Wesley STACEY
Australia born 1941
No title (Anti-Vietnam War march). 1967
gelatin silver photograph
47.1 x 39.1 cm
Purchased 1991   1991.381

Mark STRIZIC
Germany born 1928, to Australia 1949
Barry Humphries, actor, writer and satirist. 1968 from *Some Australian personalities 1967–1972*
gelatin silver photograph
38.6 x 26.4 cm
Purchased 1974   1974.428

Henry TALBOT
Germany born 1920, to Australia 1940
Gilbey's Gin. c.1967–68
direct positive colour photograph
37.4 x 35.0 cm
Purchased 1989   1989.1464

Maglia Knitwear. 1968
direct positive colour photograph
42.0 x 41.1 cm
Gift of the artist 1989   1989.294

Joe TILSON
Great Britain born 1928
Jan Palach: Suicide by fire, January 1969.
1969
colour photolithograph, collage
66.0 x 53.2 cm
artist's proof (edition 100)
Purchased 1978   1978.1030.3A–B

T — Tania la guerillera.
from *A–Z box ... fragments of an oneiric alphabet ...* 1969–70
photo-screenprint, collage
74.6 x 50.0 cm
edition 19/25
Purchased 1978   1978.1030.60.23A–B

UNKNOWN ARTIST
Australia working 1960s
Tennyson Textile Mills, Sydney
Circle. 1968
screenprinted cotton
121.2 x 119.4 cm
Gift of Sheridan Australia 1987
1988.316.26

Circles. 1968
screenprinted cotton
125.0 x 121.6 cm
Gift of Sheridan Australia 1987
1988.316.27

UNKNOWN ARTISTS
France working 1960s
Atelier Populaire, Paris
Poster: *Le chienlit c'est lui!* [*He's the freak!*]
1968
colour screenprint
38.4 x 30.2 cm
Purchased 1985   1985.2001

Poster: *La détente s'amorce.* [*The situation is easing.*] 1968
screenprint
44.8 x 56.8 cm
Purchased 1985   1985.1998

Poster: *Frontières = repression.* [*Borders = repression.*] 1968
screenprint
43.8 x 33.0 cm
Purchased 1985   1985.1999

Poster: *Non!* [*No!*] 1968
screenprint
60.0 x 47.0 cm
Purchased 1985   1985.1992

Poster: *Non!* [*No!*] 1968
colour screenprint
72.0 x 60.0 cm
Purchased 1985   1985.1997

Poster: *La police vous parle tous les soirs à 20h.* [*The police speak to you every evening at 8 p.m.*] 1968
colour screenprint
72.0 x 57.0 cm
Purchased 1985   1985.1996

Poster: *Pouvoir populaire OUI.* [*People's power YES.*] 1968
colour screenprint
98.6 x 66.5 cm
Purchased 1985   1985.2004

Poster: *Vive les occupations d'usines.* [*Support the occupation of the factories.*]
1968
colour screenprint
56.0 x 45.0 cm
Purchased 1985   1985.2002

UNKNOWN ARTIST
after **John CLEVELAND**
United States working 1960s
Poster: *Haight is love.* c.1967
colour screenprint
51.6 x 36.2 cm
Purchased 1978   1978.255.65

UNKNOWN ARTIST
United States working 1960s
after **Alphonse MUCHA**
Czechoslovakia 1860 – France 1939
Portal Publications, San Francisco
Poster for *Big Brother & The Holding Co.*
1967
colour lithograph
56.0 x 40.8 cm
Purchased 1978   1978.255.404

UNKNOWN ARTIST
United States working 1960s
Bill BRACTIS, photographer
Poster for *Moby Grape/Its a Beautiful Day/ The Other Half/Tim Hardin/Jerry Abrams.*
1969
colour lithograph
28.2 x 69.0 cm
Purchased 1978   1978.255.252

UNKNOWN ARTIST
Paul KAGAN, photographer
Poster: (*Peace sign*). c.1968
colour lithograph
57.4 x 61.0 cm
Purchased 1978   1978.255.260

UNKNOWN ARTIST
United States working 1960s
Jerry WAINWRIGHT, photographer
Poster for *Country Joe & the Fish/Pacific Gas & Electric.* 1969 colour lithograph
53.8 x 35.8 cm
Purchased 1978   1978.255.380

UNKNOWN ARTIST
United States working 1960s
Personality Posters, publisher
Poster for *Easy rider.* 1969
colour lithograph
74.6 x 101.2 cm
Purchased 1981   1981.2695

UNKNOWN ARTIST
United States working 1960s
Portal Publications, San Francisco
Poster for *Baltimore Steam Packet/Moby Grape/Only Alternatives and His Other Possibilities.* 1967
colour lithograph
56.0 x 40.4 cm
Purchased 1978   1978.255.410

UNKNOWN ARTIST
United States working 1960s
Poster: *Haight.* c.1967
colour screenprint
45.2 x 33.4 cm
Purchased 1978   1978.255.121

John VAN HAMERSVELD
United States born 1941
Poster for *Jefferson Airplane/Charlie Musselwhite/The Ceyleib People.* 1968
colour lithograph
69.4 x 49.4 cm
Purchased 1978   1978.255.41

Andy WARHOL
United States 1928–1987
Electric chair. 1967
synthetic polymer paint on canvas
137.2 x 185.1 cm
Purchased 1977   1977.795

Stamped indelibly
New York: William Katz 1967
rubber stamp print
28.5 x 21.2 cm
edition 159/225
Purchased 1983   1983.2937

Wes WILSON
United States born 1937 working 1960s
Poster for *Van Morrison/The Daily Flash/Hair.*
1967
colour lithograph
50.8 x 36.0 cm
Purchased 1978   1978.255.504

Margaret WORTH
Australia born 1944
Samsara 17. 1969
synthetic polymer paint on plywood
184.0 x 122.0 cm
Purchased 1993   1993.1934

YOKOO Tadanori
Japan born 1936
Poster for *6th International Biennial exhibition of prints in Tokyo.* 1968
colour lithograph
108.0 x 76.6 cm
Purchased 1988   1988.2251

Index of artists

Victor Moscoso *Blue Cheer/Lee Michaels/North America* 1967 lithograph